Releasing Judgment

THE PRACTICE OF *A COURSE IN MIRACLES*

THE HEALING POWER OF KINDNESS

Volume One
Second Edition

Releasing Judgment

KENNETH WAPNICK, PH.D.

Foundation for A COURSE IN MIRACLES®

Foundation for A COURSE IN MIRACLES®
41397 Buecking Drive
Temecula, CA 92590
www.facim.org

First printing, 2004
Second printing, 2006
Second edition 2011

Printed in the United States of America

CONTENTS

Preface to Second Edition

For this new edition, the book has been retypeset with increased line spacing for ease of reading. Aside from this stylistic change and the correction of typographical errors, no other changes have been made.

Preface to First Edition

The idea for this book originated with a talk I gave at our previous Center in Roscoe, New York. It came at the end of a five-day Academy class held in September 1996 entitled "Sickness and Healing," and the circumstances surrounding my talk go to the heart of this book. I do not recall the many details of the week, but do remember that our teaching staff—my wife Gloria, Rosemarie LoSasso, Jeffrey Seibert, and myself—were struck by the paradox of students on the one hand spending the week discussing healing in terms of forgiveness and undoing separation, and on the other hand fervently practicing judgment and condemnation on each other—directly opposite to our teaching (and hopefully, demonstration) and the kind, gentle tone of Jesus' words in *A Course in Miracles*. In light of this, I decided to devote the Academy's final session to talking about the kindness of healing, in the hopes of reinforcing Jesus' message of *undoing* separation by releasing judgment. Needless to say, kindness reflects our inherent oneness with each other, while attack drives us still further apart in our awareness.

Therefore, as the next volume in our series of small books on the practice of *A Course in Miracles*,[1] it seemed appropriate to address this crucial aspect of practicing the Course's kind principles of healing. The core of this book (Chapters 1, 2, and 3) is an edited transcript of the original talk.[2] It has been edited to enhance its readability, though the informal style of the original presentation has been essentially maintained. Some passages from *A Course in Miracles* have been added to expand the discussion, and some specific examples have been included that were gleaned from other classes and workshops to

---

1. The first book is titled *Ending Our Resistance to Love*.

2. Information on ordering Foundation publications appears at the end of the book. "The Kindness of Healing" is available as a single audio cassette (#T-54) and a 2-CD set (#CD-54).

illustrate how healing's kindness can be inadvertently subverted by the ego's need to separate and attack.

The Introduction is taken from the final chapter to my book *The Message of A Course in Miracles*– Volume One: *All Are Called*. It is entitled "Being Kind," and was also reproduced in our quarterly newsletter "The Lighthouse." It nicely serves to introduce the major theme of this book. Part of that chapter has been moved to this book's Conclusion. Finally, two other articles from our newsletter—co-authored with my wife Gloria—are included in the Appendix. The first, "Do No Harm to Anyone," took its inspiration from the Hippocratic oath, and served as the basis for the article's discussion of being kind and gentle. The second, "A Kind and Simple Presentation of a Kind and Simple Message" cautions students against using the Course's metaphysics as an ego ploy not to do "the simple things salvation asks" (T-31.I.2:2), which, for our purposes, we can summarize with the two-word principle: *Be kind*.

The kindness discussed in this book focuses almost exclusively on being kind to others. Volume Two, which will be published separately, focuses on the kindness of forgiving our limitations.

As always, I am very grateful to Rosemarie LoSasso, our Foundation's Publications Director, for her careful and faithful shepherding of this book from its inception, through its excellent editing to its finished form. I would especially like to thank my wife Gloria, who patiently spoke to me for years of putting out little books like these. I finally listened, and no doubt a message lies in that.

Introduction[3]

Jesus' inspirational message to the world in *A Course in Miracles*—with its beautiful language, brilliant logic, and blessed words of love—means nothing if it is not lived and practiced. This is why he makes the following important statement in the text, which can be taken as a caution to all of his students *not* to repeat the mistakes of the past twenty-one hundred years of seeking to teach his message without first seeking to learn it for themselves:

> Teach not that I died in vain. Teach rather that I did not die by *demonstrating that I live in you* (T-11.VI.7:3-4; italics mine).

In other words, we teach Jesus' message of undoing the ego's thought system of death by *living* our lives based on his teachings on forgiveness. This undoes the ego's lessons of hate, attack, and murder, and thus is the efficacy of his message demonstrated—not by our words, but by our life:

---

3. As noted in the Preface, this has been adapted from "Being Kind," the final chapter in *The Message of A COURSE IN MIRACLES* – Volume One: *All Are Called.* The closing paragraphs have been moved to the Conclusion.

> Teaching is done in many ways, above all by example (T-5.IV.5:1).

This principle of teaching what we have first accepted for ourselves is nicely articulated in the workbook lesson "I am among the ministers of God," where Jesus can again be seen encouraging his students not to make his teachings something they *do,* but rather having his students be what they seek to *become.*

> There is one major difference in the role of Heaven's messengers, which sets them off from those the world appoints. The messages that they deliver are intended first for them. *And it is only as they can accept them for themselves that they become able to bring them further, and to give them everywhere that they were meant to be.* Like earthly messengers, they did not write the messages they bear, but they become their first receivers in the truest sense, receiving to prepare themselves to give (W-pI.154.6; italics mine).

This inability to truly practice *A Course in Miracles'* kind principles of forgiveness that they study, and sometimes even teach, has perhaps been the most serious failing among its students. In *Few Choose to Listen* (Volume Two of *The Message of*

A Course in Miracles), I discuss how students often conceal their thought system of specialness and judgment under the guise of spiritual counseling or friendship. Thus, they are quick to remind someone in pain or in mourning, for example, that the body and death are illusions and defenses against the truth, and so why not, they urge their family members or friends, just change your mind. The absence of simple kindness is unfortunately unmistakable to all except the Course student making the spiritual pronouncements. In this regard I am always reminded of the classic movie *Lost Horizon*, the 1938 adaptation of James Hilton's wonderful novel. As some readers may recall, at the beginning of the film, Conway, the protagonist played by Ronald Coleman, is abducted and brought to Shangri-La, a paradisal community in the Himalayas, inhabitants of which do not grow old. He has been brought there to become its new leader, as the ancient Lama—its founder and guiding inspiration—is preparing to die. In one of the film's most memorable moments, the Lama makes a speech to the reluctant Conway, in which he explains the origin and purpose of his utopian oasis. It is an inspiring scene, and its climax comes in the following summary statement, remarkable for its prophetic words that have, sadly to say, been more than realized in the decades that have passed since they were first spoken on the screen.

It came to me in a vision long, long ago. I saw all the nations strengthening, not in wisdom, but in the vulgar passions and the will to destroy. I saw the machine power multiplying until a single weaponed man might match a whole army. I foresaw a time when man, exulting in the technique of murder, would rage so hotly with a world that every book, every treasure, would be doomed to destruction. This vision was so vivid and so moving that I determined to gather together all things of beauty and of culture that I could, and preserve them here against the doom toward which the world is rushing.

Look at the world today. Is there anything more pitiful? What madness there is, what blindness, what unintelligent leadership, a scurrying mass of humanity, crashing headlong against each other, upheld by an orgy of greed and brutality. A time must come...when this orgy will spend itself, when brutality and the lust for power must perish by its own sword....For when that day comes, the world must begin to look for a new life, and it is our hope that they may find it here, for here we shall be with their books, and their music, and a way of life based on one

4

simple rule: *Be kind.* When that day comes, it is our hope that the brotherly love of Shangri-La will spread throughout the world. Yes...when the strong have devoured each other, the Christian ethic may at last be fulfilled and the meek shall inherit the earth.

What could be simpler, and yet what is more difficult? Since our thoughts were not kind about God in that original instant of separation, all that followed in the hologram of time and space could not help being unkind: *Ideas leave not their source*— unkindness must lead to unkindness. The little willingness that Jesus repeatedly states is all that is asked of us by the Holy Spirit can best be understood as the willingness to be kind; or perhaps better, the willingness to be taught to be kind. In that ontological instant—the beginning of the ego's nightmare dream of judgment—when we placed our selfish desire for individuality above all else, kindness was lost to us and we forgot that "Kindness created [us] kind" (W-pI.67.2:4). And so we need to learn from Jesus, the one who symbolizes and exemplifies this kindness of Heaven to us, how to release judgment and be kind to others and ourselves. Hopefully, this little book will help remind us all of the need to be kind, *the* spiritual principle *par excellence.*

1. The Kindness of Healing

I would like to focus specifically on the attitude and behavior of a student of *A Course in Miracles* in the presence of someone who is sick. One would think this should not be a crucial issue. Unfortunately, however, I can assure you that in the more than twenty years [now almost thirty] since *A Course in Miracles* was published (1976), it has been and continues to be a major problem. Thus I would like to discuss it both in terms of theory and, above all, practice. While we will focus mainly on sickness, it will become obvious as we go along that the principles we examine can easily be applied to other areas as well: for example, how one deals with a person mourning the death of a loved one, having a seemingly insoluble problem, or is just upset.

As many of you know—either because you have been victims of it, or perhaps in a moment of weakness have victimized others this way—it is all too easy to deal with the anxiety engendered when you are with someone in pain by quoting *A Course in Miracles*, a nice way of saying hitting them over the head with the blue book. Its principles of help and healing then become subtle and sometimes not so subtle ways of passing judgment and attacking others. I have said many times that when you have a problem, or are sick or in trouble, the last person you should call is a Course student; and, unless that person is well trained, the last person you should go to for psychotherapy is a Course student. In all likelihood, you will only have a bunch of Course platitudes thrown at you: "What do you mean your mind isn't healed yet? I thought you were a good student! I thought you believed that this world is an illusion! Come let us pray or meditate so you can be restored to your right mind."

It has been quite a while since Gloria and I have told this story, but it remains one of our favorite unfavorite stories, and, unfortunately, a true one. A member of a Course group became gravely ill—cancer, as I recall. She was in the hospital and dying. Before her death, she was visited regularly by other members of the group, who were obviously quite upset that this long-time student of *A Course in Miracles* was sick, with cancer no less, and, even worse, was dying. Rather than do what normal friends would do for someone in pain, they quoted the Course to her, in effect saying: "If you were really serious about this Course, you would get out of that bed and come home with us. Don't you know that sickness is a defense

8

against the truth (W-pI.136)? We have a meeting tonight and would like you to be there." That last part I made up, but the point of this story is clear. Needless to say, the friend was quite hurt and upset.

Gloria and I have used this story to exemplify how easily people can fall into that trap. The mistake the group members made was not so much the unkindness and judgment toward their friend, but in not paying attention to their own anxiety: not looking at what was going on within themselves. No one could ever be unkind or withhold love unless they were first wracked with guilt and fear. That is self-evident. There cannot be anything other than love or fear in our minds, as *A Course in Miracles* tells us. We have but two emotions: one we made (fear) and one was given us (love) (T-13.V; T-12.I.9:5-6). If you have chosen Jesus or the Holy Spirit as your Teacher, anything you say or do will come from Them and will be loving. If, however, you have chosen the ego as your teacher, which means guilt and fear have taken the place of love, anything you say or do will come from guilt and fear. If you do not pay attention to the guilt, it will be repressed, and whatever is repressed will be projected. When guilt is projected, it takes the form of attack—either on yourself (sickness), or on someone else (anger). No one in his or her right mind would pretend that attack is loving.

What really happened in that group was that the members were upset that this person was a serious student of *A Course in Miracles* and yet became ill. Each one must have been thinking, "What does that mean about me? I am also a serious student, and so this could happen to me, too." The concern was certainly not about their friend, but about themselves. Again, their mistake was in not paying attention to their anxiety, and consequently using the Course as a cover for it. They thus walked into the hospital room and projected their own anxiety, which came from guilt, and in effect said to the poor woman: "You're the guilty one, and we need you to prove to us that this Course works—that if you practice *A Course in Miracles* you will never get sick. We need you to demonstrate that to us, not because we care whether you live or die, but because we care whether *we* live or die. We need you to be the proof that one can be a student of the Course and get well, and certainly not die!"

Thus, their judgmental behavior was not due to sin or wickedness, but fear, but they did not pay attention to it. That is why I stress the importance of constant vigilance for what is going on inside you. One of the general rules I always advocate is that you be normal—try to stop and think what normal people would do in a situation like this: they would be kind, gentle, and consoling, and would certainly not attack or make the patient feel guilty. From everything you have heard and read in your study of *A Course in Miracles*, you know that sickness has nothing to do with the physical symptom, but with the thought system built on our belief that we are separate from God. *That is the sickness*. The woman who was suffering in the hospital bed was obviously feeling separated, and therefore the last thing in the world she needed was for her good friends to come in and make her feel even more separated! If they had been in their right minds, they would have realized the woman's sickness and suffering was most likely coming from her fear and guilt, and her fear of dying would have found expression in her thinking: "This is God's vengeance on me and I am being punished; my individual existence is going to be snuffed out because of my sin." Whether those thoughts were conscious or not, they would have been present in her mind as the source of tremendous fear.

Once you understand the source of sickness in the mind's decision to be separate, you will realize you are joined with that person in the same sickness

No mind is sick until another mind agrees that they are separate. And thus it is their joint decision to be sick. If you withhold agreement and accept the part you play in making sickness real, the other mind cannot project its guilt without your aid in letting it perceive itself as separate and apart from you. Thus is the body not perceived as sick by both your minds from separate points of view. Uniting with a brother's mind prevents the cause of sickness and perceived effects. Healing is the effect of minds that join, as sickness comes from minds that separate (T-28.III.2).

This is why Jesus teaches over and over again in his course that if you want to be healed, you must let yourself be an extension of healing for someone else. If you want to be forgiven, you must ask his help that you forgive someone else, for only then will you understand that you and that person are the same. To state it quite simply and succinctly: when with someone, always try to be kind. Lesson 67 states: "*Kindness created me kind*" (W-pI.67.2:4). When you are acting unkindly, clearly you are acting in a way that is discordant with the way God created you.

Recall the speech of the Lama of Shangri-La that I quoted in the Introduction. When you set aside the brilliant metaphysics of *A Course in Miracles* and its sophisticated psychological insights, the Course could be pared down to the Lama's one simple rule: *Be kind.* If you are not kind, then not only are you not practicing the Course, but there is no way you can even begin to understand it. No matter how brilliant your understanding of its metaphysics may be, if you are not being kind toward another person, especially when that person is in trouble—in fear, pain, or whatever—you are not doing what this Course is asking.

A Course in Miracles helps us understand why we are not kind. If we believe we have not been kind to God—attacking Him in order to exist on our own—we inevitably believe He will not be kind to us. But we repress that threatening thought, split it off, project it out, and make a world in which we then feel justified in being unkind. That is the origin of our unkindness. However, if you do not do something about it, the unkindness remains, along with the guilt. You have to be especially careful not to mask the judgmental attacks with your Course words of kindness. In the next chapter I will talk about judgment, an important underpinning of our unkindness.

I am occasionally asked if I would say something about Mother Theresa, who did such wonderful work, but whose spirituality and theology were miles apart from the Course. I like to point out that her spirituality consisted of doing what the love of Jesus told her to do. Whatever theological terms she couched her ethic in, that was her bottom line. Compared with *A Course in Miracles*, her metaphysics and theology would clearly seem to be of the ego—it was very much rooted in the body, with Jesus being the only Son of God, the one who came to redeem us from our very real sin—but how many *Course in Miracles* students would you want to stack up against her, with all their brilliant theological and metaphysical understanding?

Again, if you really want to make progress in this course, you must practice being kind, which very often means leaving your blue book behind, but not its *author.* You do leave the words behind if they are not helpful—and many times they are not—but if you take Jesus with you, you will be as kind as he is. To repeat what I said in my opening comments, I am sure many of you, and possibly most of you—especially if you have been around *A Course in Miracles* for a while—have either been the recipient or the perpetrator of these "sinful" Course offenses of hitting people over the head with its principles. Do try to remember that if someone is in pain, dying of cancer, or even doing something unconscionable or vicious, the source of their behavior is the same fear working in your own mind—and that is what unites you. There-fore, in learning how to be kind toward another per-son, you are practicing being kind toward yourself, because you and your brother are one. You are not dif-ferent. This goes directly to the heart of the ego's thought system—the concept of difference is how the ego began: God and His Son were separate *and* different—and undoes it. It is this unconscious identi-fication with the ego's need for differences to prove its victory over God's Oneness that is the ultimate motivation behind our unkindness, especially when practiced in the name of Jesus and his course.

Q: I was with a friend whose husband had died, and she asked me how *A Course in Miracles* views death. She is not a student of the Course, but what I said made her angry, so I assume I was not being kind.

A: Not necessarily. Being kind does not always mean the other person will be accepting of your kind-ness. What is important is that you recall, as best you can, what was going on within you. Of course it is possible you were not being kind; but it is also possi-ble that you were. It is certainly impossible to judge someone else, but it is equally impossible to judge yourself and know your inner motivation. If you feel you were peaceful and not trying to conceal anxiety, anger, or fear, you need not go any further with it.

Sometimes you can be very loving toward someone and that person will still get angry. If you are in a relationship that is based on a secret vow of mutual anger and attack—marriages of that nature have lasted fifty, sixty, or more years—and all of a sudden one of the partners becomes kind and announces "I don't want to do this anymore," the other person will be very angry: "You're not acting the way we agreed! You are supposed to be miserable and nasty so I can feel unfairly treated."

Again, I don't know what your motivation was at that point, but because the other person became upset does not necessarily mean that you were being unkind. I think it is something to look at, but be kind and gentle as you do so, and don't do a number on yourself.

Q: Suppose you have two *Course in Miracles* students, one of whom is sick and the other is constantly reminding him that "this is a dream."

A: Again, it depends on the motivation. If you are reminding your sick friend that the world is a dream and sickness is a defense, you should look within yourself and try to determine whether you are coming from a loving space. If your friend is *A Course in Miracles* student, the chances are she is aware intellectually that this world is a dream and sickness is a defense against the truth. If that were the case, to remind her of that is not very loving or caring. It is like rubbing salt in the wound, or stepping on a person who is already down. Surely there are times when a reminder can be loving and helpful, but very often it is not. Again, you should always use *being normal* as a criterion. Normal people in the presence of someone who is sick, especially a friend or family member, are kind. You do not have to be a spiritual giant or understand the difference between non-duality and duality to know that if someone is sick and in pain, kindness should be offered to that person.

Similarly, it is not loving to reprimand a person who is watching a news program with you and who gets upset over scenes of bombings, genocide, or starvation: "What are you so upset about? It's all a dream. It's their script!" Sadly, there are numerous accounts of students doing just that. Anyone who makes such unloving comments must be coming from a fearful place, and rather than look within and ask

Jesus' help to deal with the fear, the person simply ignores it because it reminds them of their own hostility and threat of annihilation.

As I have been stressing, when you do not look at fear or guilt, they will automatically be pushed down in your unconscious, and just as automatically will be projected out—always. Inevitably, then, you end up judging and attacking other people. Like a stone rolling down a mountain, it is relatively easy to stop it if you get it at the beginning because it has not picked up any speed. However, if you let it roll down some distance, it becomes much more difficult, if not impossible, to stop—in fact, it becomes outright dangerous. Once your ego really gets going, it is very hard to stop yourself, because at that point you are on your spiritual high-horse, the other person is on the ground, and it feels so good to beat him up. Remember, the ego's cardinal principle is always *one or the other*, and so if I can prove that you are a poor student of *A Course in Miracles*, I clearly am the good one. That feels so good that it is more difficult to stop. Progress in the Course can be measured by the speed with which you identify your fear, not by your not having it. If you identify the fear, it won't go anywhere. But if you don't and instead push it down, it festers inside until it explodes. Thus, before you know it, you will find yourself in the throes of a major ego attack, directed either towards someone else or yourself.

What also frequently happens with people who study the Course is that they become very cliquish. There is a unique vocabulary in *A Course in Miracles*, which works fine among Course students—everyone knows what specialness and Atonement are, what it means to look at the ego, and so on—but it is not loving to use those same words and concepts when you are among people who do not know what you are talking about. It is not helpful and it certainly is not kind. When you find yourself not acting or speaking in a kindly way—when you are at a wake, for example, and you go around with a smile on your face saying to grieving friends and relatives, "Don't be upset. 'No one dies without his own consent' (W-pI.152.1:4)"— you should want to stop it as soon as you can, and then not feel guilty about it. Simply understand where the unkindness comes from, and then try to undo the cause, which invariably will be: "I wanted to be on my own and did not consult with Jesus before I went to the funeral home." You do not have to consult with him about what to say; but it is essential that you consult with him about what is going on inside you.

1. The Kindness of Healing

In one of his personal messages to Helen, Jesus said:

> Remember you need nothing, but you have an endless store of loving gifts to give. But teach this lesson only to yourself. Your brother will not learn it from your words or from the judgments you have laid on him. You need not even speak a word to him. You cannot ask, "What shall I say to him?" and hear God's answer. Rather ask instead, "Help me to see this brother through the eyes of truth and not of judgment," and the help of God and all His angels will respond (*Absence from Felicity*, p. 381).

Therefore, you do not have to ask Jesus what to say when you visit someone in the hospital, or one who has suffered a personal loss. Do ask him, though, for help in leaving your ego behind. If you cannot even do that, at least ask his help to be kind; at least try to enunciate for yourself that your goal is to be kind. Even if you sense that your ego is going wild, you can still be kind through realizing you have a split mind that is obviously divided between kindness and unkindness, Jesus and the ego, happiness and pain. Such honesty is a first step. It does not undo your ego—your secret desire to be unkind—but it does express your desire to want to do things differently.

Even though at this point you do not think you can, there still is a part of you that really wants to, and so, at the very least, you will not try to justify, rationalize, or spiritualize your unkind comments. You will, in simple honesty, acknowledge to yourself: "I said this, and obviously I was not in my right mind. I was not being gentle, kind, or loving, and did not listen to the other person. All I cared about was myself."

Q: And if you do not go through that process, you are going to feel guilty and rejected.

A: Absolutely. And feeling guilty will impel you to attack again and again and again. That is what we refer to as the guilt-attack cycle—the ego's bread and butter. The guiltier you feel, the more you will project it out and perceive yourself as the innocent one, justified in attacking the guilt you see in others. Yet the more you attack, the guiltier you will feel. Thus the cycle continues, and nothing ever changes. Once again, you can at least express to yourself, to Jesus or the Holy Spirit, your desire to be kind: "I don't know how to be kind, but that is my goal—to be kind, gentle, caring, and loving." If you can sincerely do that, even when you start to judge or spout Course platitudes, you will no longer attempt to justify what you are doing, and will realize you are not being kind at all.

Q: Can we do this in other circumstances—even if someone is not physically ill?

A: Yes, of course. I am using physical illness as the primary example, but you can apply this whenever you are with someone one who is upset—for any reason—including yourself. Remember, the sickness is not the physical symptom. Sickness is the expression of the belief: "I am separated from God, and prefer my individuality to the Oneness of Christ." Regardless of why someone is not at peace—whether it is a physical, emotional, financial, or relationship problem—it is still the same sickness, for it comes from the same source of separation.

A student from New York told me of his experience with other Course students after the 9/11 attacks. He was talking with them about how traumatic it had been dealing not only with his own fear and distress, but also with frantic relatives who were frightened for the safety of their children who were in school, and for spouses who were at their jobs in Manhattan, or stranded on business trips in other parts of the country, etc. After sharing these experiences, one of his

Course friends said, "Oh, I didn't take it seriously. I knew what it was about—I knew that it was meaningless and that it was all an illusion." Needless to say, he felt he had just been judged a Course failure, even though his friend did not say that explicitly.

If your mind is healed of the belief in the illusory world of separation, there would be nothing there but the kind, gentle love of Jesus, and therefore there would never be a need to announce that you know attack and fear are illusory. You would be sensitive to the fear in others, and not separate yourself from them by tacitly letting them know that you have advanced far beyond where they are. Granted, most people do not usually let go of the belief in separation in one single instant of healing. More commonly, they learn how to take themselves and the events of their lives less and less seriously. Still, though, kindness would dictate that they at least be present to the pain in others, and try gently to comfort them, rather than exacerbate the problem through playing the game of spiritual one-upsmanship.

Another example of the unkindness of insensitive students of *A Course in Miracles* came during one of our workshops in Roscoe. Shortly before dinner, discussion in the class focused on one student who related still another Course horror story. She had some

23

cardiac problems, which medication helped to allevi-
ate, and she was sharing her experience with her
weekly group. To her hurt and amazement, a number
of her "friends" began to attack her for resorting to the
magic of medicine rather than the Course's miracle of
healing. She was accused, in characteristic ego
fashion, of not being a good student, etc. Her bringing
this up in my workshop allowed me to discuss many
of the ideas already expressed in this book, and the
session ended with the woman feeling considerably
relieved. At some point during dinner, however, she
came up to me, practically in tears. While waiting in
the cafeteria line for her food, *the very same thing
happened all over again.* A participant in the session
that just ended approached her with the exact same
accusation. Unlike Heraclitus' ever-changing river,
some things never change. Or so it would seem.

To cite another example shared by a student in one
of my classes, we can even be unkind toward ourselves about our unkindness to others! A student, Pat,
was having a problem with Alice, a woman living in
her neighborhood. When Alice would see Pat in the
park, where they both would go regularly, she would
sit next to Pat and begin to talk. Pat found the conver-
sation terribly boring, and also intrusive on her relax-
ation time. So Pat wanted to know if she were still

being a "good Course student" if she didn't want to talk to Alice. Sometimes Pat would stay and talk, but feel resentful about it, and other times she would get up and leave, thinking that was all right to do, but then later feel guilty about having left. After all, Pat berated herself, Alice is just as much a member of the Sonship as she is. Pat wanted to know whether it would be more loving to stay and pretend she were interested in what Alice had to say, even though she was not.

My response to Pat centered on two of the basic points we have already touched upon: First, the importance of always being normal, and second, the problem is never what is happening in the world (the *form*), but always with one's choice of the ego rather than Jesus as one's teacher (the *content*).

We all have our preferences of likes and dislikes: food, colors, personality types, music, hair styles, movies, climates, and so on. That is a fact of our existence in this world as bodies, and has nothing to do with our spiritual status. Therefore, we need but acknowledge our preferences without making them into an issue. Pat could simply have recognized that she preferred not to spend time with Alice, without hating or judging her, and certainly without making the situation into some kind of cosmic spiritual test, which she appeared to have failed. Pat essentially crucified herself by thinking: "I should be able to be with anyone and talk about anything." The kind and gentle approach would have been to have simply acknowledged: "This is the self I think I am. I like food A; I like movie A; I prefer to be with person A." In that spirit, Pat could simply have excused herself and then sat somewhere else or gone back to her apartment, and she would have remained peaceful throughout. Pat was not peaceful, however, which means she chose the ego as her teacher instead of Jesus. Her decision not to stay with Alice became a sin, for which she felt terribly guilty—always a sign of having chosen the ego. That was Pat's mistake. It was not her not wanting to be with Alice; it was her choosing the ego as her teacher.

Being in a body already means we have chosen the ego's thought system of *one or the other*. So Pat could have realized "If I didn't want to be with God, why would I want to be with this woman?" In other words, there is no difference between Pat seeing herself as separate from God and seeing herself as separate from Alice. Our judging against others is no different from our judging against God—it is just a shadowy fragment of the "tiny, mad idea." This echoes the first principle of miracles, that there is no order or hierarchy among them (T-1.I.1:1), which undoes the ego's first law of chaos, that there is a hierarchy of illusions (T-23.II.2:3). Had Pat joined with Jesus instead of the ego, she would not have judged herself for excluding Alice from her love, but she also would not have justified excluding her; and finally she would have recognized that seeing Alice as separate was an obstacle to her experiencing the peace and Love of God that is within her. So kindness toward herself would be manifested in forgiving herself for not being perfect in her love for all people—her humble acceptance of her limitations and not attacking herself because of them. Jesus does not care about *form*—about whether or not you spend time with persons A, B, or C. He cares about *content*—what is going on in your mind—whether or not you exclude people, including himself—*in your mind.*

As I have indicated, our assumption that we can rightly judge both ourselves and others is what fuels our unkindness, and so I would like now to turn to some passages in *A Course in Miracles* that speak directly to this underlying and infectious dynamic. The equally damaging confusion of form and content will be highlighted as well.

2. Judgment and the Belief in Differences: The Basis of Unkindness

"How Is Judgment Relinquished?"

A favorite activity of many students of *A Course in Miracles* is self-righteously judging others in the name of the Course itself. Thus, they reason, if someone is sick, it is obviously because of their guilt—we have been praying for them and they still have their symptoms; that obviously means they are guilty! However, when you think about it, how could they possibly know the meaning of the symptoms in the greater Atonement path of that person? They base their answer entirely on form—what their eyes see— and have no idea of what is going on in the person's mind. Thus, again, they cast judgment in the guise of being a good student.

I will read something now from "How Is Judgment Relinquished" (M-10), which states in the clearest of terms that such judging is impossible. This is not the only place in *A Course in Miracles* where Jesus talks about the impossibility of judging, but it is perhaps the most explicit. Jesus' point is that we cannot judge or understand anything. Therefore, whenever we feel we are superior Course students and justified in our judgments—always on the basis of external data—of where others are on their Atonement path, think of these passages.

(M-10.3:1) The aim of our curriculum, unlike the goal of the world's learning, is the recognition that judgment in the usual sense is impossible.

Jesus is not talking only about condemnation, the obvious meaning; he is also using the broader sense of judgment: understanding anything at all—judging where a person is on his or her spiritual path, for example.

(3:2-7) This is not an opinion but a fact. In order to judge anything rightly, one would have to be fully aware of an inconceivably wide range of things; past, present and to come. One would have to recognize in advance all the effects of his judgments on everyone and everything involved in them in any way. And one would have to be certain there is no distortion in his perception, so that his judgment would be wholly fair to everyone on whom it rests now and in the future. Who is in a position to do this? Who except in grandiose fantasies would claim this for himself?

This is self-explanatory, and so I will continue—it gets a little worse.

(4:1) Remember how many times you thought you knew all the "facts" you needed for judgment, and how wrong you were!

Anyone who has even a slight degree of self-honesty would realize how true this is.

(4:2-3) Is there anyone who has not had this experience? Would you know how many times you merely thought you were right, without ever realizing you were wrong?

Forget about the times it was clear you were wrong—how about all the other times?

(4:4-5) Why would you choose such an arbitrary basis for decision making? Wisdom is not judgment; it is the relinquishment of judgment.

That describes the Course's objective. Its curriculum is all about the giving up of judgment, "the obvious prerequisite for hearing God's Voice":

> The world trains for reliance on one's judgment as the criterion for maturity and strength. Our curriculum trains for the relinquishment of

judgment as the necessary condition of salvation
(M-9.2:6-7).

Early in the text Jesus tells us of the rewards of not
judging:

> You have no idea of the tremendous release
> and deep peace that comes from meeting your-
> self and your brothers totally without judgment
> (T-3.VI.3:1).

**(4:6–5:5) Make then but one more judgment. It is
this: There is Someone with you Whose judgment
is perfect. He does know all the facts; past, present
and to come. He does know all the effects of His
judgment on everyone and everything involved in
any way. And He is wholly fair to everyone, for
there is no distortion in His perception.**

**Therefore lay judgment down, not with regret
but with a sigh of gratitude. Now are you free of a
burden so great that you could merely stagger and
fall down beneath it. And it was all illusion. Nothing more. Now can the teacher of God rise up
unburdened, and walk lightly on.**

You should re-read these paragraphs whenever
you are tempted to judge others—not only in attacking and finding fault with them, but also in presuming

to know where they are spiritually, or what their physical symptoms mean.

Sickness can be thought of as judgment, as I mentioned earlier—the original judgment that says I know what is best for me; God does not know, I know, and I am better off being on my own: autonomous, free, and independent of Heaven. That is absolute madness, and all judgments we have ever made come from that insane thought, and everything that has followed from that first judgment shares in that insanity. Think about the fact that the actual phenomenon of perception is judgment:

> Perception selects, and makes the world you see. It literally picks it out as the mind directs.... Perception is a choice and not a fact (T-21.V.1:1-2,7).

In order to perceive something, we have to perceive it relative to something else—figure against ground, the ground being the background and the figure being whatever is focused on. If we do not have that contrast, we cannot perceive. Thus we select out of our entire perceptual field what we are looking at and listening to, and automatically screen out what is irrelevant to us. Thus, for example, the people in this room who are looking at me and listening to what I am saying are screening out other auditory and visual stimuli. On the other hand, if there is someone in the room who is here not as a student of *A Course in Miracles* but as an interior decorator, for example, that person would be perceiving the color of the walls, the shape of the room, and the general ambiance. What I am saying and reading would be in the background. We all must perceive something here, otherwise we cannot function as bodies, and therefore we are always separating what is important from what is not important—and that is a judgment.

We can say, then, that our entire physical universe is based on separation and judgment, all stemming from the original judgment we made as one Son that individuality was preferable to Heaven's Oneness. Obviously we made the wrong judgment and wrong choice, and consequently everything that has ever followed from that has been equally wrong.

"Make then but one more judgment." The only judgment we *should* make is that we made a mistake, and that there is Someone within Who can help. What the Holy Spirit will tell me about my sick friend has nothing to do with my sick friend. He will talk to me about *me,* so I can realize that if I am concerned and am making judgments, it is because I am not paying attention to my innate sickness. Therefore, my Teacher, Who is also my Healer, will call attention to my sickness and help me realize that if I join with Him I will no longer be sick. Since He is beyond judgment, I too will be beyond judgment when I join with Him. The peace and love within me would be unaffected by what is happening in my friend's body, because I will now know that my friend and I are joined with the Holy Spirit. At that point anything I say or do will be loving, because it will have come from the loving right-minded space in my mind.

Before you say or do anything, before you judge or think anything, you should first make sure that *you* are no longer sick. Again, sickness is judgment, and has nothing to do with physical symptoms. It is needful, therefore, that you pay careful attention to when you are judging. Be aware of it, realizing you are allowing someone else's circumstances to have an effect on you, which means, again, that you are now the one who is sick. This is the symptom you should be looking at and judging against—but not out of guilt. This form of judgment says, "I made a mistake, and there is Someone within me Who will look at me differently and therefore will help me look at this person differently." The help is not so much about being able to look at that person differently as much as it is about seeing what *you* are doing. The Holy Spirit would help you realize that what you are seeing in this other person is what you do not want to see in yourself. If you are anxious, fearful, depressed, or guilty because of someone's illness, problem, or circumstances, there is something unhealed in yourself that you were not aware of, but is now rising to the surface in search of suitable victims of your projections. You need to stop everything you are doing and go within and be healed. The way you are healed, to state it again, is to ask Jesus or the Holy Spirit for help in looking at what is truly making you so sick, which can always be reduced to the same thing: you want to be right, and you want to be on your own.

Jesus talks about gratitude frequently in *A Course in Miracles*, especially emphasizing that we should be grateful for all situations that make us the most uncomfortable, because without them we would not know there is something unhealed in us. Thus if you are upset over what is happening with someone, you understand now—through having Jesus instruct you—that this person has become the screen onto which you have projected some guilt that you do not want to look at in yourself, and thus see in another. This is the secret wish our projections hide:

> It [the world] is the witness to your state of mind, the outside picture of an inward condition (T-21.in.1:5).

> [Perception] is the outward picture of a wish; an image that you wanted to be true (T-24.VII.8:10).

Exposing that wish to have the image of your sinful brother be true is the gift your relationships bring you. That is what Jesus means by saying that your brother is your savior, not because of anything he is doing or saying, but simply because your relationship with him is providing the opportunity of looking at something in yourself you were not looking at before.

Q: If I have worked through a lot of judgment with another person and am peaceful, when I go back to my ego, will all of the murderous thoughts return?

A: Yes. The ego is a 100 percent thought system—it does not decrease. It is hatred and murder through and through, and therefore if you are back in your ego system, you are back into hatred and murder. What changes as you progress in the Course—and there is no objective way of measuring this—is the amount of time you spend in your ego, as opposed to the amount of time you spend with the Holy Spirit. When you are in your ego, it is the full-blown ego. Similarly, when you are with Jesus, there is only love, because there is nothing else. All that changes is the amount of time you choose to spend being insane—it might be twenty-three hours a day and you get it down to twenty-two and three-quarters. I am being facetious, of course—it is not really quantitative—but it is the time we spend with hate or love that changes.

Thus, you could have worked through a lot of hatred toward someone, so that you now see this person as your companion on the journey, no different from you. Then all of a sudden you become frightened and fall back into the ego and pick a fight. What might be different now is that you are aware that you just became frightened, and your current state is different from how you were before. Your attack, therefore, may not be as intense, or the frequency and duration not be as great as what it used to be. However, when you are with your ego, you are in totally, and become hateful, vicious, and mean. What would change is that you will not believe in it quite as strongly as you used to. Something is missing—the oomph is not there, because part of you knows it is made up.

Q: Can all of these techniques or concepts be applied to ourselves when we are sick?

A: Yes, absolutely. In fact, that is an excellent place to practice. A typical reaction when a student of *A Course in Miracles* becomes sick is to try to analyze the guilt, thereby judging it. Remember the familiar line from Chapter 18, where Jesus says:

> You are still convinced that your understanding is a powerful contribution to the truth, and makes it what it is (T-18.IV.7:5).

Jesus does not think much of our capacity to understand! The idea is not to try to understand why you are sick or what is going on, other than to know that whatever is going on in your body or in your life is coming from the sickness of believing you are better off on your own. *That* you should know, because Jesus does teach you that here. Once you understand that your sickness is that you pushed Jesus and his love away, it will be obvious that your healing lies in inviting him back in. It is very simple. Whether you judge yourself or others, it is the same sickness. As I say repeatedly, because Jesus says it repeatedly, that is why this is a simple course—every problem is the same, regardless of the form, and so every solution is the same, regardless of the form. Therefore, this works for yourself as well as for your perceptions of others.

Healing As the Undoing of Separation

I want to read a line from the *Psychotherapy* pamphlet in the section called "The Definition of Healing." I make a point of reading it when I give a workshop on psychotherapy. It is a remarkable statement about healing in that it says absolutely nothing about the patient. Jesus has just stated that the final goal of psychotherapy is the realization that unforgiveness is the only problem and therefore forgiveness is what heals. Then he asks how this goal is reached, and answers. This is one more place where Jesus tells us in one sentence how his course is learned, and what it takes to achieve its goal. And now he tells all therapists, which includes all people, how they reach this final goal of forgiveness:

> The therapist sees in the patient all that he has not forgiven in himself, and is thus given another chance to look at it, open it to re-evaluation and forgive it (P-2.VI.6:3).

That is how psychotherapy heals, how a relationship heals, how a teacher of God heals. Notice again that Jesus says absolutely nothing about the patient: "The therapist sees in the patient all that he has not forgiven in himself." Implied in this, of course, is that because the therapist has asked Jesus for help, he has another chance to look at what was secretly buried in him, because he now is seeing it in someone else.

Thus, becoming upset or bored with your patient, or concerned about a friend who is dying of cancer or AIDS, or who has just stubbed his toe, is a red flag signaling you that there is something unhealed in you, and that you now have another opportunity to re-evaluate it and assess your values and priorities. Looking with the help of Jesus is what makes forgiveness possible. Nothing is said about judging the patient—making the patient feel guilty. Everything is said, though, about having the therapist healed. In fact, the entire pamphlet is about that, because once the therapist's mind is healed, he will allow the true Healer to heal through him.

The therapist's role is not to be brilliant in his judgment of someone else, anymore than it is your part to be brilliant in analyzing why someone is sick or not getting better. Your job is simply to be aware that your concern about someone else is a projection of some-thing unhealed in you. Once aware of that, you then have a meaningful basis for asking help of Jesus—not for help in looking at the other person differently, or for help so you would say the most loving thing, but for help to forgive yourself. At that point, then, every-thing you say will be loving and kind.

As an illustration of these principles, I would like to refer to a discussion I had many years ago with a professional couple, David and Anne, who worked in a mental hospital. Our discussion came during my workshop on "Healing the Unhealed Healer." They wanted to review with me how they had been dealing with administrators in the hospital who they thought were making a serious mistake in their approach to patients. David and Anne felt it was part of their responsibilities to help correct this administrative situation.

The goal of the administration was to make money, not to help people, which should come as no surprise to anyone; and that involved unspoken policies such as keeping patients in the hospital longer than needed because their insurance had not run out yet. That was a fairly common way for the hospitals to make money—again, not a surprise. Clearly, on the level of form, this is not helpful; and just as clearly, on the level of form, David and Anne's attitude was an attempt to be helpful, because their concern was to help their patients. There was one flaw—a serious one—in their argument, however, and that is what I would like to talk about.

Again, on the surface (the form), they appeared to be doing the right thing. Yet beneath the surface it became equally clear that something else was going on: they, in effect, wanted to kill the administration! That is a slight exaggeration, but the content is there, even if the form is muted. That, incidentally, is one of the signs of an unhealed healer: the belief that the form is important. David and Anne's mistake was in forgetting that the reason they were in the hospital was not to heal the patients that were referred to them. The reason they were working in the hospital was to heal the administration. They were just going about it in the wrong way. When viewed on the level of content, healing is joining. David and Anne had conceived of their work as joining with the patients, but as poor victims who desperately needed their help. These patients were not only victimized by their circumstances, they were also victimized by the hospital administrators, who were now seen as the bad ones, as opposed to the good ones: namely, David and Anne, and everyone else who cared about them.

What David and Anne forgot, what we all forget, is that our purpose is to join, but that the joining is never on the level of form, but only on the level of content. That means that we cannot join with one person or one group if we are allied against another. Joining with one in opposition to another is the perfect way of appearing to be engaged in healing, but doing the exact opposite. That is what *The Song of Prayer* pamphlet calls "healing-to-separate" (S-3.III.2:1): I am the healer and I have something you do not have; I am seeing you and me as separate, but yet I am attempting to help you. In that sense these healers ultimately believe they are gods, with the power and knowledge to dispense healing when and where they choose, forgetting that

> God does not know of separation. What He knows
> is only that He has one Son (P-2.VII.1:11-12).

And each one in David and Anne's situation — administration, staff, patients—is part of the one Son of God. To exclude one is to exclude all, since God's Son cannot be divided and remain as God created him.

Thus, David and Anne were attempting to heal by joining with the patient group, but they were separating themselves from the administration through their judgments. Healing could not take place then. What they did was to split their perception of the Sonship into good versus bad. And it happened because they got caught in the trap, as we all do, of mistaking form for content. They felt that their job was to do what they were trained to do, which was to heal the mentally ill. But that is not the job Jesus "assigned" them. That is what they were paid to do by the world, but he wanted them to heal their minds of the belief in separation. Once that is accepted as your goal and only purpose and function, it is clear that if you are involved in a cause that is pitting you against someone else—where your point of view, which differs from another point of view, becomes paramount—all you are doing is continuing to split and separate. And that means you are doing the exact opposite of what you really want to be doing. Not only, then, can you not be an instrument of healing for the person outside you, you also obviously cannot be healed yourself.

This works with everyone, whether you are being paid as a mental-health worker in one form or another, or you just see yourself as a helper of others. It works for whatever you are involved with. When you believe what is important is the task—which always implies that you know better than someone else—that is another clear sign that you are listening to the ego. Now on some level you may feel you know better. For instance, if someone you are with says 2 plus 2 equals 5, you will say no, 2 plus 2 equals 4. There is a part of you that knows that *you know* that 2 plus 2 equals 4, but then you don't make it into a big deal. That is the issue. As I have said numerous times, *A Course in Miracles* is not teaching us to deny that there are differences. It is teaching us not to make the differences into a big deal.

And so David and Anne clearly would say—and find countless others who would agree with them, no doubt—that they are right: that the most loving thing to do is to discharge a patient who is ready to go home, and not have their medical insurance be a factor. But they are wrong, because what they are really doing is separating themselves from the administration. In the section entitled "The Correction of Error," Jesus says the Son of God is never wrong—his ego may be wrong, but our job is still to tell him he is right (T-9.III.2). Of course that does not always mean on the level of form. It is not helpful to a third-grade student to be told he is right in thinking 2 plus 2 equals 5—that is not going to help him function in the world. But there is a way of telling him 2 plus 2 equals 4 without also telling him that *as a person* he is wrong. You do not have to attack. Before you correct someone's error, you first want to be sure that your mind is joined with that person's mind.

So again, David and Anne's task was to join with the administration first. If they do not, they are not going to be of help to anyone in the hospital. They then would just continue to separate and separate and separate. The issue is not what David and Anne *do* (the level of form). The issue is that within themselves (the level of content) they not harbor grievances and side with one group against the other. Remember, anyone who is in this world is automatically wrong, and so to take sides is to say some groups are more wrong than others; that there *is* a hierarchy of illusions. To do that is to be wrong still again. We are all wrong in the same way, and we are all right in the same way.

Therefore, if you become aware that you are looking to pick a fight—to polarize a situation—realize that you are doing this to keep yourself away from the Love of God, and then ask yourself if this is really what you want. The answer is obvious. If you are serious about wanting to be joined with the Love of God and to feel that peaceful Presence, the only way that is possible is to join with the people you have made into the enemies. Be aware that you are pushing them away, because that is a way of pushing God away, and you don't want to do that any more. At that point it would be much more difficult to justify being angry. What is really necessary is to totally rethink the purpose of your life. Whether you are working in a hospital or in General Motors does not matter. What is needed is a total rethinking, re-experiencing, and restructuring of why you are here. You are here simply to undo the thoughts of separation in your own mind and release your judgments, and the form does not matter. If you want to be of help, then you must experience a joining and not a sense of opposition. That is what is behind those very important lines in the text, "Trust not your good intentions. They are not enough" (T-18.IV.2:1-2).

3. On Being a Teacher of Kindness

We turn now to the subsection called "The Function of the Teacher of God" (M-5.III), which focuses on our function as advanced teachers of God, those who have already progressed far enough along the path that they, like Jesus, kindly represent the Atonement to others. The previous two sections of this chapter addressed our recognizing that sickness is not in the body but in the mind. Now Jesus asks:

(M-5.III.1:1) If the patient must change his mind in order to be healed, what does the teacher of God do?

For the purpose of our discussion, we will regard the teacher of God as anyone in the presence of a person who is sick, upset, or troubled with problems.

(1:2-3) Can he change the patient's mind for him? Certainly not.

Your job is not to convince others that their sickness is a defense against the truth; nor is it to change people's minds so they understand that the world is a dream, and they are its dreamers, dreaming of sickness, anger, and death.

(1:4-13) For those already willing to change their minds he has no function except to rejoice with them, for they have become teachers of God with him. He has, however, a more specific function for those who do not understand what healing is. These patients do not realize they have chosen sickness. On the contrary, they believe that sickness has chosen them. Nor are they open-minded on this point. The body tells them what to do and they obey. They have no idea how insane this concept is. If they even suspected it, they would be healed. Yet they suspect nothing. To them the separation is quite real.

We may know the theory very well—that we are never upset for the reason we think, for instance (W-pI.5)—but Jesus is telling us that our function is not to change people's minds. We are not trying to convince them that *A Course in Miracles* is a better spiritual path than the one they are following. Likewise, we are not trying to remind them, if they are Course students, what they have forgotten. This is our purpose:

(2:1) To them [those who are sick] God's teachers come, to represent another choice which they had forgotten.

Your only function is to be a reminder to others that they can make the same choice you did—not necessarily through words, but through the love and peace you demonstrate to them.

(2:2-3) The simple presence of a teacher of God is a reminder. His thoughts ask for the right to question what the patient has accepted as true.

The patient—really all of us—has accepted the ego's thought system as true. To us, individuality is not only a value; it is an accomplished fact. From individuality come sin, guilt, and fear, and our personal and collective worlds. We accept it all as true because we have forgotten where we come from; all we know is that we are here as bodies, burdened with a seemingly endless array of problems. We never even question the basic premise on which our existence rests: namely, that this world is real.

When you are in the presence of those whose minds are healed, they say to you, even though it may not be in words: "The same choice I made you can make, because our minds are one." To repeat this important caution, most of the time you would never actually say these words. Love's presence, which is outside the ego's thought system, is what teaches— not by your words, but by the teacher you have chosen in your mind. You teach by the presence within you. *What* you teach does not matter. You could be teaching *A Course in Miracles* and get every theological point correct, but if there is no love in your heart, you are not teaching *A Course in Miracles*. Before you teach verbally, you want to be clear it is your Teacher teaching through you. As Jesus says in the beginning of the manual, everyone teaches all the time (M-in.1-2), but we are teaching either from the ego or the Holy Spirit. When you are not being kind—that is, when you judge, or try to change someone's mind or life—you are coming from your ego. Change is good to the ego. That is what got us here. On the other hand, change also becomes a tremendous symbol of guilt and anxiety for the very same reason: change is what got us here. The ego will get you both ways. But the one thing the ego never wants you to do is change your mind!

> Many stand guard over their ideas because they want to protect their thought systems as they are, and learning means change. Change is always fearful to the separated, because they cannot conceive of it as a move towards healing the separation. They always perceive it as a move toward further separation, because the separation was their first experience of change. You

believe that if you allow no change to enter into your ego you will find peace (T-4.I.2:1-4).

(2:4-6) As God's messengers, His teachers are the symbols of salvation. They ask the patient for forgiveness for God's Son in his own Name. They stand for the Alternative.

The "Alternative" is the Holy Spirit—the abstract, non-specific presence of Love, the Atonement, the memory of God in our minds. You may recall Jesus saying that the Atonement principle was in effect from the beginning, but it needed an act in order to set the plan in motion, which established Jesus as its leader (T-2.II.4:2-5; C-6.2:4). This is meant meta-phorically, for a non-specific God can have no specific plan with a specific leader. Yet because we believe we are specific, we need something specific to symbolize for us the abstract love in our minds. The specific plan of the Atonement, with Jesus as its specific leader and teacher, is the correction for the ego's specific plan of separation, guilt and attack:

> Complete abstraction is the natural condition of the mind. But part of it is now unnatural. It does not look on everything as one. It sees instead but fragments of the whole, for only thus could it invent the partial world you see. The

> purpose of all seeing is to show you what you
> wish to see. All hearing but brings to your mind
> the sounds it wants to hear.
>
> Thus were specifics made. *And now it is specif-*
> *ics we must use in practicing* (W-pI.161.2:1–3:2;
> italics mine).

Jesus is thus the specific expression of that abstract
love, as is his course. Since he is the Holy Spirit's
manifestation, he asks us to be his manifestation in the
world as well (C-6.1:1; 5:1-4). We are asked throughout the Course to be the specific expression of that
abstract love, and you may recall from the Introduction this wonderful line from the text where Jesus
says: "Teach not that I died in vain. Teach rather that
I did not die by demonstrating that I live in you"
(T-11.VI.7:3-4). The way we teach the truth of the
resurrection principle has nothing to do with Jesus'
body. The resurrection takes place in the mind, when
we awaken from the dream of death, which means
that Jesus did not die. In fact, no one can die because
no one has lived—there is no life within the dream.

Therefore Jesus tells us that we teach his resurrection, not through pronouncements or mastering the
metaphysics of *A Course in Miracles*, but by demonstrating that he lives in us. What does that mean? It

means that his love is what motivates, guides, and inspires us, and radiates through us. That is how the truth of the Course is taught. To say it still one more time, if you are not kind to someone, you are telling that person that Jesus is dead—and if he is alive, he certainly is not alive in you; and if he is not alive in you, he cannot be alive in anyone else—we are one.

It is your kindness that teaches far, far better than any mastery of the intricacies of the ego thought system. Kindness is what heals. Remember, sickness is separation and has nothing to do with the body. Don't try to judge the state of mind of others by the state of their body, because you have no way of understanding the role that that particular body has in the person's overall Atonement plan. As we saw in the previous chapter, only Someone Who is outside time and space, Who knows the whole plan and has a command of the entire hologram can see how everything fits in. There is no way anyone here can know that. Thus, the minute you try to evaluate someone according to their body, or according to what they do or say, or do not do or do not say, you become the sick one. *Sickness is not of the body.* Sickness is of the mind that believes in separation, that believes not only in judgment but also that its judgment is correct. As we read:

> The miracle is useless if you learn but that the body can be healed, for this is not the lesson it was sent to teach. The lesson is the *mind* was sick that thought the body could be sick; projecting out its guilt caused nothing, and had no effects (T-28.II.11:6-7).

By denying a person's experience of a physical or psychological problem, we deny them the only hope for change—the power of their minds. The sick body is the window that opens to the sick mind, offering another chance to choose again. Kindness facilitates this choice; judgment prevents it.

It is important to be clear about what Jesus is teaching. He is not simply telling us that we should not judge; indeed, he wants us to understand that judging is impossible because we have no means of making valid judgments. Instead, he wants us to become a symbol of the Alternative, by the love and peace within us. If there is love in us, others will experience it in us, whether they consciously accept it or not. *When* they choose to accept it is up to them. Recall that lovely passage relatively early in the text where Jesus says:

> I have saved all your kindnesses and every lov-
> ing thought you ever had. I have purified them of
> the errors that hid their light, and kept them for
> you in their own perfect radiance. They are be-
> yond destruction and beyond guilt. They came
> from the Holy Spirit within you, and we know
> what God creates is eternal (T-5.IV.8:3-6).

It is your love that says to another person: "There
is another way. There is something else within you."
Once we identify with that something else, everything
we say or do will come from that love. Even if we are
simply quoting from the phone book, it will not make
any difference. It is not the form but the content, as
Jesus will say below.

**(2:7) With God's Word in their minds they come in
benediction, not to heal the sick but to remind
them of the remedy God has already given them**.

In *A Course in Miracles*, the *Word of God* is almost
always associated with the Atonement: forgiveness,
the Holy Spirit—anything that expresses the Correction for the ego's thought system. When we have
joined with Jesus in a holy instant, we become one
with him; and as he tells us in the text, he is the Atonement, which is God's Word, and he is the correction,

because he represents the fact that the separation from God never happened (T-1.III.1:1; T-8.V).

If you try to heal the sick, you are making external sickness real, which means you are paying no attention to the true sickness in the mind—our having made the wrong choice. Standing within the holy instant, I say to you by my love and my peace: "There is another choice. There is a remedy in your mind that will remind you of the Love of God, and that you did not separate from Him." Again, what my body does or says is irrelevant. It will do and say whatever is the most helpful: a kind word or gesture, medical or psychological intervention, wise advice.

(2:8-9) It is not their hands that heal. It is not their voice that speaks the Word of God.

It is the love and peace that is in your mind that speak the Word of God, which has nothing to do with the words coming from your mouth or your body's activity. Of course, if putting your hands on someone (the laying on of hands) is a way of manifesting the Love of God to a person who is receptive to that form, by all means do it. Just do not be fooled into thinking that the behavior is the healing. Likewise, if saying a prayer with someone helps that person, do it. Again,

58

don't make the mistake of thinking the prayer is what heals.

Jung told the story of himself when he was working in a mental hospital in his early years. There was a woman with whom he got absolutely nowhere in his treatment. She was very regressed and would just sit in her room—it probably was a cell—and nothing that this brilliant psychiatrist could say to her did any good. Finally, in his humility, he said to her one day, "You know, nothing I am doing is helping you; what do you suggest?" She replied: "Read the Bible to me." Jung was the son of a minister who was not very loving, and he had very little use for the Bible. But the woman said, "read the Bible"; so he did. She left the hospital soon afterwards.

Jung told that story as an example of how a psychiatrist does not know anything. But he did know to do what the woman said would help her. And the woman was right. It was not the words of the Bible that healed her; and Jung especially did not believe in what he was reading. But what he did was express love and help in the only form that the woman could accept; a form that was the only helpful thing he could do at this point, because everything else he thought would help did not. His kind joining on the level of the mind expressed itself in his reading the Bible to a woman who believed in it.

Along these same lines, a man in one of my classes spoke about his experience with a friend who was dying:

> He asked me to pray with him. It was very difficult, in the sense that I wanted to be sincere in what I said and did with him. I truly wanted to pray for some miracle to cure him; and he prayed for "magic." It was very difficult for me to join him in that, but I did anyway, knowing that what I was praying for was for the fear of him passing to go away. So I have been wondering if I was of service to him; was I of any help—because it wasn't genuine.

I responded:

> I think you made it complicated, because you mixed up form and content. The form was that your friend believed in magic and wanted a magical God to intervene, and you had a conflict about that. The issue really had nothing to do with that. All your friend was asking for was that you join with him. Now he may not have consciously thought that, but that's what he really wanted, which means the content was that you

join with him. He made it very easy for you. He was basically saying, all you have to do is pray in this way. The conflict was that you kept hearing the form instead of the underlying content. If you had heard the content, you would have prayed with him without any conflict. You would have read the Bible to him every day, and you would have said all kinds of prayers, written letters to God, Santa Claus, or anyone he wanted you to write letters to. This was his way, his vocabulary—the only way he could understand that you loved him and you were one with him.

This is the same idea as the passage in *A Course in Miracles* that says if your brother asks you to do something outrageous, do it [T-12.III.4]. Well, your friend asked you something outrageous. He asked you to perform magic. And as that passage in the Course says, you experienced a strong sense of opposition, which meant you were being just as magical as he was. He believed that your praying that way would save him, and you believed *not* praying that way would save him. And the issue is not how you pray at all—in terms of form. He was actually telling you the form—and if you listen, everyone will tell you what they need, in the form in which they need it.[4] That's because they are too afraid of the content's bottom line: God is. Well, no one wants that! That's too terrifying. That's what love is. It doesn't do anything—it's pure content, non-specific. But we have to have that non-specific, abstract love be translated to us in a form that we are comfortable with. And if you listen, people will tell you the form. So your friend told you the form he needed.

The reason you hesitated and experienced conflict is that you, too, were afraid of the love. It had nothing to do with the form, the theology of prayer, or anything else like that. You were simply afraid of the love. This fear is what causes us not to be able to hear other people's calls for love, and we then immediately jump to the form: "I won't do that; that's not spiritual." Yet what is spiritual is hearing someone's call and meeting them there in the form they can accept without being afraid.

That confusion of form and content is always where students get trapped, which accounts for those awful stories about what students say: "I'm

---

4. I recently gave a workshop based on that theme called "Healing: Hearing the Melody." It is available on CD (#CD-88 4 CDs). For ordering information see the end of the book.

not taking you to a doctor. The body is an illusion. If I take you to a doctor, I'm enabling your ego." What you are really doing is wishing them dead!—but calling it something else; you are disguising it and hiding it by deceit. If people are in pain, they are saying the only way they can accept love is to have you take them to the doctor. The most loving thing you can do is honor their request and take them, not give them *A Course in Miracles* lecture. You hear the call, and the call comes in a form, because we are creatures of form. But you use the form to reflect the underlying content, which never changes.

To summarize, people will make it very easy for you if you just listen. They will tell you what they need. And if you experience resistance, it is not because the form does not agree with you; it's because the content terrifies you. And then you use the form as the excuse not to exemplify the content, which is love.

Let me read some lines that are particularly relevant to these examples and to what Jesus is saying in the manual. They appear early in the text, in Healing as Release from Fear":

> The value of the Atonement does not lie in the manner in which it is expressed. In fact, if it is

used truly, it will inevitably be expressed in whatever way is most helpful to the receiver. This means that a miracle, to attain its full efficacy, must be expressed in a language that the recipient can understand without fear. This does not necessarily mean that this is the highest level of communication of which he is capable. It does mean, however, that it is the highest level of communication of which he is capable *now*. The whole aim of the miracle is to raise the level of communication, not to lower it by increasing fear (T-2.IV.5).

Jesus' message is that even though you may believe *A Course in Miracles* contains the holiest words ever written, saying them to another person is not always helpful. Indeed, chances are that if someone is in distress, the words of the Course would *not* be helpful. The love that inspires the words is always helpful, however, but not necessarily the words themselves. To restate this crucial point, if a friend of yours is *A Course in Miracles* student and is sick, then clearly that person understands that sickness is a defense against the truth, that sickness really is guilt, and on and on and on. Therefore, there is a part of him that would feel guilty because he is betraying the Course, and now he is going to be punished for his failure by death. However mistaken he is in thinking that, he still feels that way. Thus for you to quote the Course to him is the very worst thing you could do, because it will merely increase his fear and make him even guiltier that he is not doing what Jesus is telling him he should do. What is really happening is that *you* are not doing what Jesus tells you to do. *You* are not being kind, and are increasing the person's guilt and fear rather than diminishing it. In your arrogance, you may even think *you* are capable of "the highest level of communication," but the other person is not. When you make someone more fearful or guilty, you obviously are not acting kindly.

"It is not their hands that heal. It is not their voice that speaks the Word of God." It is not the form of what you do that is important; it is the love with which you do it that heals. Not that love has any magical power, for all it does is remind the person who is sick that there is another choice. Anyone who believes he or she is separate from God and is in a body is sick! Remember, the purpose of *A Course in Miracles* is to restore to our awareness the power of our minds to choose. That is why at the end of the very first chapter in the text, Jesus says "this is a course in mind training" (T-1.VII.4:1). Its purpose is to remind us that our minds are extraordinarily powerful. We have the power to choose to believe we have destroyed Heaven —not that we *can* destroy Heaven, but we have the power to *believe* we did. As a reaction to that belief and the resultant guilt, we have repressed our power, and therefore it lies buried in our minds. We thus need something such as *A Course in Miracles* to teach us how to bring it to awareness. Once we do that—by choosing the right Teacher—we will be in a position to be a model and an example for others. We would be demonstrating they can make the same choice we did. You need not say a word about the Course, God, spirituality, or about the mind and body. You simply need be loving. Of such kindness is the Kingdom of Heaven on earth.

(2:10) They merely give what has been given them.

What has been given us is love. Remember, we have but two emotions—one we made and one was given us (T-13.V.10:1). Love and fear have coexisted in our minds but have been split off. We now are able to see they were both there. We choose against fear and for love, accepting what God has given us. And we now serve as models for the choice that others can make.

(2:11-12) Very gently they call to their brothers to turn away from death: **"Behold you Son of God, what life can offer you. Would you choose sickness in place of this?"**

This is what we say, not in words but in content. By my caring, kindness, and love I offer you an example of what you can choose instead of pain. I do not make you choose it, and I do not make you feel guilty if you do not. I offer you another opportunity of seeing that it is possible to experience yourself in this world with the growing understanding that you are not of this world, which means for the first time you will have a sense of hope that you can be happy, not by changing your circumstances here, but by changing your mind about those circumstances—your interpretation and reaction to them. I have done it at least in this instant, which shows you that it is possible.

As I demonstrate this to you and to others, I strengthen it in myself; so that when I forget and become afraid, and in my insanity believe I am better off being separate from love, I now have a reference point in myself I can turn to. I can remember: "You know, when I chose Jesus and chose against the ego I felt better. All that has happened now is that I have again become insane, fearing the loss of this miserable, puny thing I call myself. I am holding on to nothing!" That sane choice I now represent to you.

(3:1) Not once do the advanced teachers of God consider the forms of sickness in which their brother believes.

Whether a person has a splinter, cancer, or AIDS makes no difference, because the sickness has nothing to do with the body. The ego's first law of chaos is that there is a hierarchy of illusions (T-23.II.2). So if the ego thought system directs my thinking, I will not make a person who has stubbed his toe feel guilty because he forgot about Lesson 136; but if a person has cancer, I will really sock it to him, because cancer is serious! Jesus is teaching us the mistake in that kind of thinking: a body is a body is a body, whether you have a stubbed toe or a tumor: "Not once do the advanced teachers of God consider the forms of sickness in which their brother believes."

An advanced teacher of God knows and understands, having learned from the Holy Spirit that sickness is of the mind and is nothing but the decision: "I know best. My judgment is not only real, it is wise; and I am happiest when I am on my own and not with God." An advanced teacher recognizes the sickness and then recognizes the symptoms of the sickness. Simply by believing you are a body makes you sick, whether your body is normal, healthy, and functioning perfectly, or is breaking down. There can be no judgment among levels of sickness (the form the body takes), except in insanity.

(3:2) To do this [believe in a hierarchy of illusions] **is to forget that all of them** [all forms of sickness] **have the same purpose, and therefore are not really different.**

Throughout *A Course in Miracles*, Jesus empha-sizes that purpose is everything (e.g., T-17.VI.2:1-2; W-pI.25,29). The wrong-minded purpose of being born in a body, dying of cancer, AIDS, or a heart attack, or being hit by a car is always the same: to prove that God is wrong and I am right. The form makes no difference. Yet these "calamities" can serve the right-minded purpose of forgiveness, if we allow the Holy Spirit to teach us.

(3:3) They seek for God's Voice in this brother who would so deceive himself as to believe God's Son can suffer.

The way that you, as an advanced teacher of God, seek for God's Voice in your brother is to see with the eyes of Jesus. He looks beyond the forms to the thoughts of guilt and separation that are protected by the forms, and then beyond the thoughts of guilt and separation to the love that is his only reality.

(3:4) You then remind your brother that he did not make himself, and must remain as God created him.

Remember, the fundamental ego thought, the premise of its thought system, is that I made myself—I am my own creator, the author of my reality.

So you will reach God's Voice in your brother to the extent that you are not fooled by the forms of his defenses: his body and everything going on within it. You understand that the body's activities—any problem the person is experiencing—has been chosen as a defense against the guilt in that person's mind, which was chosen to protect his individuality; and that choice was a defense against the Love of God. Thus you see through the layers of defenses, which now become to you but flimsy, fragile veils that lack the power to conceal the light (T-18.IX.5:4; T-29.IV.4:11; W-pI.138.11:3). To the ego these defenses are as "solid granite" (T-22.III.3:4), not allowing you to get beyond them. When Jesus is your teacher and you have his eyes, you look right through the thoughts of sickness. You do not deny them, but by understanding the nothingness they are, you look beyond them to the light they were defending against.

In sum, the guilt in our minds is a shield against the love in our minds, and our bodies are shields against the guilt. At that point it does not matter what form the body is in—perfect health or falling apart. A body is a body is a body! It is mere illusion, a defense against guilt, and guilt is a defense against love.

(3:5) They recognize illusions can have no effect.

Our bodies, let alone the sickness and problems they experience, are the seeming proof that illusions have effects. The illusion of being separate from God, called sin, leads to guilt and fear, and to a world that is their effect. But if I do not take the effects seriously, which means I do not give them power to take away the love or the peace of God—specifically, I do not give your sickness or your problem power to take away the love and peace of Jesus within me—I am saying to you that your illusions of being separate from God have had no effect on me. Once again, I become an example of what you can achieve, for if the understanding that "illusions can have no effect" is within me, it is also within you, because our minds are joined. That is how forgiveness works and sin is undone. If sin is shown to have no effect, it cannot be a cause; and if something is not a cause, it does not exist. Your belief in sin—being separate from God—has no effect on me. If it has no effect on me, it is not a cause. If it is not a cause, it does not exist, which means it was all made up. Jesus expresses this in the lovely line from "The Little Hindrance": "Not one note in Heaven's song was missed" (T-26.V.5:4). Separation had no effect, and therefore never happened.

(3:6) The truth in their minds reaches out to the truth in the minds of their brothers, so that illusions are not reinforced.

This statement says nothing about *my* reaching out. *I* do nothing. It is *the truth in me* that reaches out. In reality, it does not even "reach out." God's Son is one, and therefore when my mind is healed—in that holy instant of complete identification with the Holy Spirit or Jesus—I am one with the Sonship. *Reaching out* is the same idea as God extending Himself and creating Christ. It is not a spatial phenomenon. The term suggests something spatial—extending outward —but when God extends His Love and gives birth to Christ, as it were, Christ does not then have an existence outside Him:

> What He creates is not apart from Him, and
> nowhere does the Father end, the Son begin as
> something separate from Him (W-pI.132.12:4).

This cannot be understood by a mind identified with a
body that is trapped in a dimension of time and space.
However, as Jesus says in discussing God's last step:

> This is true, but it is hard to explain in words be-
> cause words are symbols, and nothing that is true
> need be explained (T-7.I.6:4).

Similarly, the truth reaching out from one person to
the truth in another is not really a reaching out. Truth
does not go anywhere. Its oneness simply is.
A Course in Miracles is written this way because we
still experience spatial separation: I am here and you
are there. Once we understand that minds are one, we
know that truth does not reach out. Its very nature is
to encompass the mind of the Sonship. Removing the
blocks to this extension constitutes healing. There are
a number of places in the text where Jesus, in talking
either about forgiveness or the miracle, says the same
thing; namely, that our task is to choose the miracle or
forgiveness, but their extension through us is not our
concern (e.g., T-16.II.1; T-27.V.1; T-28.I.11). We do
not do anything. If you think you are doing something,

or are concerned about what happens to someone else, your mind is sick and cannot be kind, let alone heal.

You may recall that further along in the manual, in the section titled "Should Healing Be Repeated?" Jesus explains in a very challenging statement that if you are concerned that someone has not been healed by you, your concern is not what it seems to be: it is really hate:

> One of the most difficult temptations to recognize is that to doubt a healing because of the appearance of continuing symptoms is a mistake in the form of lack of trust. As such it is an attack. Usually it seems to be just the opposite. It does appear unreasonable at first to be told that continued concern is attack. It has all the appearances of love. Yet love without trust is impossible, and doubt and trust cannot coexist. And hate must be the opposite of love, regardless of the form it takes. Doubt not the gift and it is impossible to doubt its result. This is the certainty that gives God's teachers the power to be miracle workers, for they have put their trust in Him (M-7.4).

Your concern should be simply to get yourself out of the way. As Jesus says at the end of the workbook in a beautiful passage, our concern is only with giving welcome to the truth (W-pII.14.3:7). We give welcome to the truth by letting go of the interferences to it.

(3:7) They are thus brought to truth; truth is not brought to them.

Illusions are brought to truth; truth is not brought to illusions. When you try to heal someone's sickness on the level of form, or when you are concerned about someone's sickness and judge it, you are bringing truth to the illusion. This accomplishes nothing but preventing truth from healing the illusion.

Jesus and the Holy Spirit are not in the body or in the world. They do not look at physical symptoms, and you should be very grateful they do not. They are the healing principle in the mind, where the sickness is. Thus, again, you bring the illusion to the truth; in other words, when you have Jesus' help and look through his eyes, you will see through the illusion of the thought of sickness to the truth itself. But you must look at the illusion first and release your judgments; otherwise choosing against it has no meaning.

(3:8) So are they dispelled, not by the will of another, but by the union of the one Will with itself.

It is not *your* will, brilliance, or healing energy, not the radiance of *your* aura, the hot blast of energy from *your* hands, or *your* ability to quote the Course chapter and verse that does anything. Indeed, *you* are irrelevant. As long as you think you are special, you obviously are as sick as the other person. Your task, once again, is to get yourself out of the way. What heals is "the union of the one Will with itself." In the holy instant, when your mind is sane and you are with Jesus and identified with his vision, you represent the unity of the Sonship. That is what heals—the remembrance that the Sonship is one and has not been separated.

(3:9) The function of God's teachers is to see no will as separate from their own, nor theirs as separate from God's.

Recall the example of David and Anne, and how their lesson was to learn that no one in their situation—administration, staff, or patients—was separate from anyone else.

Again, healing is the experience, however brief it may be, that the mind is one; and if the mind of God's Son is one, there is no separation; no sin, guilt, fear, world, body, and sickness. What is so difficult, as students say all the time, is to give up our identification with the body. We think we live within it and that if we do not get enough to eat or enough oxygen to breathe, something bad will happen. It is extremely hard to understand, and certainly to experience, that we are not our bodies. That is why this takes a lot of hard work, and a lot of gentleness and kindness towards others and ourselves. You need to be gentle with yourself, understanding and respecting your own fear, let alone the fear of others.

Importantly, none of these teachings should be taken to mean that you should not pay attention to what other people are saying to you, or that you ignore their suffering. The heart of the teaching is that you not let circumstances, however awful they may be, affect the love and the peace of Jesus within you. If you can do that, you cannot but be kind to everyone—not just to *specific* groups or *specific* people on *specific* days depending on their *specific* symptoms or *specific* circumstances. You will be kind to *everyone, all the time*, because there is only kindness within you. Obviously, you cannot manifest kindness to each of the five billion people on the planet, but you can, in your mind, not exclude anyone. You will demonstrate that kindness to whoever is part of your classroom—and you do not choose who is in and who is not. The bottom line always is to let Jesus be your teacher; for then it will be his eyes through which you see, and his love through which you act and speak. He says in the Introduction to the fifth review in the workbook:

> For this alone I need; that you will hear the words I speak, and give them to the world. You are my voice, my eyes, my feet, my hands through which I save the world (W-pI.rV.in.9:2-3).

The world that is saved is the world of the sick mind that believes it is separated. As long as that sick mind believes it is a body that interacts with other bodies, the healing thought of love must be expressed in the specific form we believe we are in: the world and the body. Our job then, when our minds are healed, is to be present to other people in whatever form or on whatever level they are comfortable with, but to know that we are not really there, that we are *in* the world but not *of* it. Our identity and our reality at that moment is with the mind and its love, which represents the oneness of God's Son. That is the message we want to give.

Q: It makes us feel so peaceful and loving to be in our right mind, so why doesn't it last?

A: Why can't we make that peace and love last, if it is so wonderful? Because there is a part of our mind that is insane, that does not believe that peace and love are wonderful. Remember, the ego began in the instant the Son decided to run away from peace and love and choose conflict. Indeed, the ego thought system is built on conflict: I killed God, and now He is going to rise from the dead and kill me. The foundation of our world is the thought that I can escape from conflict. I project it from the mind, and now my body is in conflict with everything. My very existence as an ego, thus, is built on conflict. You cannot have conflict and be with peace and love. The idea, then, is to realize the mistake in choosing conflict and pain over peace and love. Once you have had an experience of peace and love, you would find it much more difficult to take your ego seriously. But there is still a part of you that says, "You'd better watch it! If you keep on with this Jesus fellow, you are not going to be your self any more."

Q: God knows what I will be!

A: Right! That's the problem! The fear is that if you keep this up, you will lose your identity. But when you have the experience of love, and in that experience all your problems are gone, it becomes almost impossible in the long run to take your problems quite so seriously again. This is also the basis of the fear of getting well that many people experience. The first part of the section of the manual we were discussing describes healing from the point of view of the wrong mind, where, in relation to God, sickness and pain are valued for the strength they confer on suffering:

> And what, in this insane conviction, does healing stand for? It symbolizes the defeat of God's Son and the triumph of his Father over him. It represents the ultimate defiance in a direct form which the Son of God is forced to recognize. It stands for all that he would hide from himself to protect his "life." If he is healed, he is responsible for his thoughts. And if he is responsible for his thoughts, he will be killed to prove to him how weak and pitiful he is. But if he chooses death himself, his weakness is his strength. Now has he given himself what God would give to him, and thus entirely usurped the throne of his Creator (M-5.I.2).

In other words, if my identity is built upon sickness and problems, healing means letting go of my ego identity, in back of which is the "terrible" truth that

God was right and I was wrong. Thus healing, as the above paragraph states, reflects that I am responsible for my thoughts, and if so, no one else is, which means that God is going to get me. I am therefore much better off being sick, because then I can say to God: "Look, you don't have to punish me; I've already suffered enough." That is a clever, but vicious ploy of the ego that basically tells God: "Butt out! I don't want your love. I also don't need you to punish me because *I* am going to punish me." Therefore, I want to stay sick. And so, letting go of the symptoms becomes a great threat.

We close this chapter on being a teacher of kindness with this lovely quotation from the text. I have taken the liberty of changing four words:

> Teachers of kindness, each in his own way, have joined together, taking their part in the unified curriculum of the Atonement. There is no unity of learning goals apart from this. There is no conflict in this curriculum, which has one aim however it is taught. Each effort made on its behalf is offered for the single purpose of release from guilt, to the eternal glory of God and His creation. And every kindness that points to this points straight to Heaven, and the peace of God. There is no pain, no trial, no fear that kindness

can fail to overcome. The power of God Himself supports this kindness, and guarantees its limitless results (adapted from T-14.V.6).

What better way to structure our day than to remember this unconflicted curriculum of kindness, the gentle, non-judgmental path to Heaven and the peace of God.

Conclusion

"A Jesus Prayer" – Jesus As Our Model of Kindness

Emulating our Creator's kindness and Love, and striving to be kind to one another here—born of our choice not to see anyone's interest as separate from our own—we reflect our mind's decision to be willing to learn how mistaken we were in believing that by withholding love we would be made stronger. Learning to accept Jesus' consistent kindness *to* us, we would wish only to have that same kindness be extended *through* us. As he tells us:

> Hold out your hand, that you may have the gift of kind forgiveness which you offer one whose need for it is just the same as yours. And let the cruel concept of yourself be changed to one that brings the peace of God (T-31.VII.5:6-7).

The simple rule of the Lama of Shangri-La—*Be kind*—should also be the guiding principle of students of *A Course in Miracles* seeking to learn and practice Jesus' teachings of forgiveness. In this way, our self-centered belief in the need for anger and judgment is undone, replaced by the loving kindness that Jesus has always held out to us. In the beautiful prose poem *The Gifts of God*, we read Jesus' comforting words as he urges us to take his kind gifts of mercy in exchange for our cruel gifts of hate:

> Give me these worthless things [things of slander] the instant that you see them through my eyes and understand their cost. Then give away these bitter dreams as you perceive them now to be but that, and nothing more than that.
>
> I take them from you gladly, laying them beside the gifts of God that He has placed upon the altar to His Son. And these I give to you to take the place of those you give to me in mercy on yourself. These are the gifts I ask, and only these. For as you lay them by you, reach to me, and I can come as savior then to you. The gifts of God are in my hands, to give to anyone who would exchange the world for Heaven. You need only call my name and ask me to accept the gift of pain from willing hands that would be laid in mine, with thorns laid down and nails thrown away as one by one the sorry gifts of earth are joyously relinquished. In my hands is everything you want and need and hoped to find among the shabby toys of earth. I take them all from you and they are gone. And shining in the place

where once they stood there is a gateway to another world through which we enter in the Name
of God (*The Gifts of God*, pp. 118-19).

With these thoughts in our hearts and prayers on
our lips, we continue our journey with Jesus, offering
kindness to the Son of God who is both our brother
and our Self. *A Course in Miracles* provides the perfect structure for this journey: Jesus the comforting
hand that steadies our steps along the way, and kindness the daily principle that helps us remember Who
walks beside us along the road that leads from specialness through forgiveness, and on to the peace of God.

As a close, I would like to read one of Helen's
poems that fits in very nicely with everything we have
been discussing. Many of you know it, for I read it frequently. This is a prayer from us to Jesus—that we
become like him. The poem ends with the more specific prayer, that when we are with people and they
look on us, they will not see us, but only him.

The idea that I began with—of being kind—is an
expression of Jesus' love. Thus everyone's prayer
ought to be that they become the specific expression
of the peace and kindness he so lovingly exemplifies.
If you choose that as your goal, you would always
have a model to follow when you are with someone:

"Am I kind the way Jesus would be, or am I judgmental?" If the latter, I am saying to this person: "When you look at me you will not see Jesus; you will see *me*: an expression of God's wrath, not His Love—because my judgment, which is righteous and valid, is the way God judges you." Your question to yourself should therefore be: "Is this the way I want to be seen? Or as an expression of Jesus' kindness and love?" "A Jesus Prayer" can guide you through the rest of your life, as you happily learn to let go of judgment and become, like him, a teacher of kindness.

The poem begins with the phrase, "A Child, a Man and then a Spirit," and the capitalization indicates the words refer to Jesus. Two stanzas later the same lines appear, "A child, a man and then a spirit," without the capitalization, because they represent us. The meaning of the poem/prayer, therefore, is that we grow to become like him. Experiencing his love leads us to demonstrate it to everyone else—kindness extending kindness to kindness. Thus is the world healed in our elder brother's kindness and love, which will one day be ours, for it is already our own:

A Jesus Prayer

A Child, a Man and then a Spirit, come
In all Your loveliness. Unless You shine
Upon my life, it is a loss to You,
And what is loss to You is also mine.

I cannot calculate why I am here
Except for this: I know that I have come
To seek You here and find You. In Your life
You show the way to my eternal home.

A child, a man and then a spirit. So
I follow in the way You show to me
That I may come at last to be like You.
What but Your likeness would I want to be?

There is a silence where You speak to me
And give me words of love to say for You
To those You send to me. And I am blessed
Because in them I see You shining through.

There is no gratitude that I can give
For such a gift. The light around Your head
Must speak for me, for I am dumb beside
Your gentle hand with which my soul is led.

I take Your gift in holy hands, for You
Have blessed them with Your own. Come, brothers, see
How like to Christ am I, and I to you
Whom He has blessed and holds as one with me.

A perfect picture of what I can be
You show to me, that I might help renew
Your brothers' failing sight. As they look up
Let them not look on me, but only You.

(*The Gifts of God*, pp. 82-83)

APPENDIX

Do No Harm to Anyone[5]

The source of our title is the ancient Hippocratic oath, which dates from the fourth century B.C. It contains one of the cardinal principles of all medicine, summarized in these five "little" words: *Do no harm to anyone*. This statement can also be used as a succinct reminder for all students of *A Course in Miracles* who seek to apply its principles to living in the world.

In this article we shall go from the general principle *Do no harm to anyone* to its specific expressions in surveying how we can better understand and implement the purpose of the above statement. We can begin by asking ourselves: Exactly what does it mean to me not to harm anyone, and moreover, how can I live my life based and patterned on this principle? A thorough examination of what I call my life must now ensue, for I must begin to look at *all* my assumptions, beliefs, values, and modes of being in this world. This process, undertaken with sincere purpose, will uncover and yield astounding information and

5. Reprinted, with minor modifications, from the September 1998 issue of *The Lighthouse*.

insights about how I function and relate to other persons in my life. And as a student of *A Course in Miracles*, the context for this exploration will be what Jesus teaches us about projection, specialness, and relationships. At first, it may quietly dawn on me that I have used other persons in my life to fulfill my desires, and satisfy my needs and wishes. Is this harmful? Well, let us look at a few examples and try to determine what is underneath the pattern:

1) Let us say I have used others to get ahead in school, at work, or in any endeavor. I am really taking what I need from them in order to advance myself, and I do not really care about giving them anything in return, nor do I even care about their well being at all. Basically, then, my attitude is a very selfish one, filled with self-interest. But I conceal my true intentions behind an attitude of respect and friendliness. The end result is that I am being dishonest with others and myself about my true purpose in these relationships.

2) In romantic relationships, I perhaps can glean how I have used other people to satisfy my emotional and/or physical needs, not caring if I might have caused harm by lying about my true intentions so as to cover the secret intent of the relationship.

3) In my family relationships I may realize that in growing up I had a need to excel and be the best in

everything so that my parents would shower their praise on me to the exclusion of my siblings. In other words, I had to use and manipulate all the situations that arose within my family as the means to extract love, approval, and praise from them, so that my star would shine the brightest among all the others in the family. I never really cared about my parents or my brothers or sisters *for themselves*; my concern was simply for what they could do for me so that I might achieve my goal of specialness.

Looking back on these three examples, it becomes abundantly clear that I have used relationships in my life to satisfy myself, with no consideration being given to the welfare of others. *And this is indeed harmful!* The thoughts and deeds listed above include omissions of love and commissions of selfishness, greed, and self-interest, all of which are encompassed by *A Course in Miracles*' term *specialness*. I realize that I have been very harmful to myself and others because my mode of being in the world came from scarcity and lack, the hallmark of the ego's wrong-minded thought system. Many realizations follow, such as:

a) If I believe I am a body, then the ego will always be my teacher because it teaches that we are all separate bodies that are incomplete, requiring something from the outside to complete us. This necessitates my taking from you what I need to fill my own perceived lack.

b) Harming others—this comes from a misunderstanding of who I am, who you are, and what the purpose of life is. Relating as an ego will always cause harm, always be harmful, and result in harmfulness. That is a given. But since I have never taken the time to reflect on my thoughts, words, or deeds prior to this time, I was never aware that I could exist as a harmful being, unknown to myself, but perhaps not to others.

c) Using people for my needs is really an attack on them, which, *A Course in Miracles* teaches, only engenders guilt in myself and keeps me stuck in my wrong mind. My anger is always directed at you for your failure to meet my needs, and for not fulfilling the function I have given you in the dream I call my life. As Jesus states in the text, in a section called "Dream Roles":

> In simplest form, it can be said attack is a response to function unfulfilled as you perceive the function.... When you are angry, is it not because someone has failed to fill the function you allotted him? And does not this become the "reason" your attack is justified? (T-29.IV.3:1;4:1-2)

Finally, I see that this guilt-attack cycle has pervaded all my relationships, even though I was not aware of my unconscious dynamics. Furthermore, it now occurs to me that I have never allowed anyone to be intimate and close to me because of my strong need to defend myself. And what am I defending myself *from*? Obviously, I did not want people to use me as I had used them. And so I unconsciously erected an emotionally aloof pattern of relating to this world, so that no one could ever get close to me. This is what *A Course in Miracles* refers to as the *attack-defense* cycle:

> Attack, defense; defense, attack, become the circles of the hours and the days that bind the mind in heavy bands of steel with iron overlaid, returning but to start again. There seems to be no break nor ending in the ever-tightening grip of the imprisonment upon the mind (W-pI.153.3:2-3).

It is now clear to me that a great part of my life has been overshadowed by *harm*; not only because of my prior discoveries about myself and relationships in general, but also because in all my doings I constantly was judging everyone—as if they were totally separate and distinct from me. So, through judgment, I made separation real, and indelibly imprinted it on my mind. Using rationalization of judgment as a sign of maturity and knowledge just kept the guilt in place. Why? Because *projection makes perception* (T-21.in.1:1). I take the guilt I believe is within me and place it on another, and then judge that person for it. A *Eureka* moment occurs—I finally realize that I have used the written word for attack. Correspondence with others over the years, to use one example, has caused me much harm, let alone the others who were the objects of my projection and attack. Unconsciously, I have used the written word as an instrument of doing harm. There is almost a cascading effect of self-discovery as I begin to generalize from the specific harmful thoughts, words, and deeds I have become aware of, and now can see the more general pattern of projection and attack that has permeated all my relationships in life. As I press the *pause* button on my self-reflection, the thought surfaces: "What does it mean to do harm by *omission?*"

With pen in hand, I can begin to jot down probing questions about omissions in my life. Some of the thoughts are as follows:

1) Have I failed to accept responsibility in any of my relationships?

2) Have I also used my emotionally aloof pattern of relating as a means of being passive in all my relationships?

3) Have I chosen not to see what is before my very eyes, because I have made a prior decision not to let anyone else infringe upon my independence?

4) Have I made a prior decision to wall off part of the Sonship as having nothing to do with me under the guise of a justified *xenophobia*?

5) Another helpful recognition surfaces: one cannot have real relationships if they are based on need; and how difficult it is to set needs aside!

6) Last, but certainly not least, have I omitted kindness and caring from my repertoire of thoughts and behavior? Except, of course, when it would serve my specialness needs. This part of my self-examination will also have a ripple effect as the search continues to seek and find what is blocking me from fulfilling the principle: *Do no harm to anyone.*

In the manual for teachers, under *gentleness*—the fourth characteristic of a teacher of God—we interestingly enough do not read very much about being gentle, but do find stated there a great deal about harm and the need to set aside this primary thought in the ego's arsenal of specialness and hate. Indeed, the word *harm* (and its derivatives) appears nine times in the two-paragraph sub-section, while *gentleness* (and its derivatives) appears only three times. This is not surprising since the overriding emphasis in *A Course in Miracles* is on the *undoing* of the ego thought system as the pathway home to God, the Source of all Love. Taking a few lines from the opening paragraph, we can see this important emphasis on a teacher of God letting go of the thought system of harm:

> Harm is the outcome of judgment. It is the dishonest act that follows a dishonest thought. It is a verdict of guilt upon a brother, and therefore on oneself. It is the end of peace and the denial of learning. It demonstrates the absence of God's curriculum, and its replacement by insanity (M-4.IV.1:3-7).

Thus, Jesus is explaining to us how our judgments of others are preceded by our judgment of ourselves. Following the dictates of the ego, we first believe that there is something inherently wrong with us, because we have produced and manifested a dream wherein the content states: "I have accomplished the separation from my Creator and Source." Then, horrified by the guilt over such wrongdoing, we seek to escape its pain by first denying that it is in ourselves, and second, projecting it out, making someone else guilty of what we have first accused ourselves of having done.

Thus, the *dishonest thought* is our self-accusation, and the *dishonest act* is our accusation and judgment of another. And by placing a *verdict of guilt* upon our brother, we are merely reinforcing the guilt we first made real within ourselves. It inevitably leads to *the end of peace and the denial of learning* because we have called upon the ego to be our teacher, thereby blotting out *God's curriculum*, and replacing it with the insanity of wrong-minded thinking. To continue with the passage:

> No teacher of God but must learn,—and fairly early in his training,—that harmfulness completely obliterates his function from his awareness. It will make him confused, fearful, angry and suspicious. It will make the Holy Spirit's lessons impossible to learn. Nor can God's Teacher be heard at all, except by those who realize that harm can actually achieve nothing (M-4.IV.1:8-11).

The first sentence in the above passage is very emphatic and all-encompassing in its application. It states unequivocally that a student of *A Course in Miracles* must learn *fairly early in his training* that harmfulness must be totally undone, otherwise he would never learn the Holy Spirit's lessons. In other words, notions of harmfulness as expressed in thought, word, or deed of any kind, will immediately cement us into the wrong mind, even though we may believe otherwise. It will block us from ever becoming aware of our intentions and motivations, both conscious and unconscious. And since we can see that inherent in the Course's process of undoing is to make the unconscious conscious—in order to become aware of our ego so it can become undone for us by the Holy Spirit—what we are doing by holding on to harmful and judgmental thoughts is effectively sabotaging our study and practice of *A Course in Miracles*. A final realization must be that harmful thoughts block out the Holy Spirit's Voice, thereby ensuring that we shall never awaken from the dream and return to our Source.

In conclusion, I can now understand what it means not to harm anyone, *with no exceptions*. To live one's life based on this principle means that in all circumstances, relationships, events, and situations, I must constantly monitor my thoughts and sensitize myself to discern when I have left my right mind—home of the Holy Spirit—and made a decision to switch to my wrong mind—the domain of the ego. This is no small task, since most of us lead lives of habitual responses to ego programming as a natural way of relating. Having spent more time with the ego as our friend, it would seem unnatural for us to relate truly to Jesus or the Holy Spirit as our Teachers. And to let go of harm—in any way, shape, or form—can seem like an insurmountable task. But as a quick reminder, *A Course in Miracles* states that all we need is *a little willingness* to let go of *our* way and *our* perceptions, and ask for the Help of Harmlessness that is always there for us. And so let us recall Jesus' words on *gentleness* from the manual, reminding ourselves that it is *his* hand we wish to take, as together with him and all our brothers we walk the gentle way of *Do no harm to anyone*, paraphrasing workbook Lesson 195 as we go, *Love is the way we walk in harmlessness*.

> Therefore, God's teachers are wholly gentle. They need the strength of gentleness, for it is in this that the function of salvation becomes easy. To those who would do harm, it is impossible. To those to whom harm has no meaning, it is merely natural. What choice but this has meaning to the sane? Who chooses hell when he perceives a way to Heaven? And who would choose the weakness that must come from harm in place of the unfailing, all-encompassing and limitless strength of gentleness? The might of God's teachers lies in their gentleness, for they have understood their evil thoughts came neither from

God's Son nor his Creator. Thus did they join their thoughts with Him Who is their Source. And so their will, which always was His Own, is free to be itself (M-4.IV.2).

A Kind and Simple Presentation
of a Kind and Simple Message[6]

Readers accustomed to seeing articles in our news-letter that deal with metaphysical issues, will be sur-prised at this one. Our basic emphasis here is why we as students of *A Course in Miracles* persist in *not* doing the *simple things* salvation asks (T-31.I.1:10– 2:2), thereby rejecting the wonderful benefits that the Course is offering to us, and through us to others. Moreover, the simplicity of its message goes hand in hand with the kindness that is inevitable if one truly practices forgiveness—clearly the heart of the mes-sage. In the following article, therefore, we focus on how this simple message falls prey to the lethal barrier of our choice for the ego thought system, which results in our core need to judge and attack others. In the spirit of this non-metaphysical simplicity, we take our cue from Jesus' opening words to Workbook Lesson 133, "I will not value what is valueless.":

---

6. Reprinted, with minor modifications, from the June 2000 issue of *The Lighthouse*.

> Sometimes in teaching there is benefit, particularly after you have gone through what seems theoretical and far from what the student has already learned, to bring him back to practical concerns. This we will do today. We will not speak of lofty, world-encompassing ideas, but dwell instead on benefits to you (W-pI.133.1).

Therefore, in dealing with everyday life situations, a revealing way to monitor our minds in practical matters that we find difficult, is to watch how we respond when our families, friends, or even ourselves are going through periods of crisis or stress. It is at these times that unconscious feelings of self-condemnation relentlessly surface in projected judgments about how we or those in pain are not good students, or are "not doing it right." The tendency at that point might be to lecture someone, or to think we have failed the Course ourselves. And, no doubt, we all have experienced, either directly in ourselves or in others, the use of metaphysical platitudes—distorted versions of the actual Course teachings—resulting in hostile projections. Unfortunately, Shakespeare's famous line from *The Merchant of Venice*—"The devil can cite Scripture for his purpose" (I, iii)—has found truth in *A Course in Miracles* circles as well. Incidentally, Jesus echoes this statement in the Course itself (T-5.VI.4:4). The following are some examples, unfortunately all taken from actual events, of such "loving" comments of Course students:

Why are you taking that pill or going to the doctor? Simply change your mind.

Why do you weep at your loved one's death? Have you forgotten that death is unreal?

Why do you remain in your hospital bed? Read Lesson 136 ("Sickness is a defense against the truth.").

How can you institute a lawsuit? You are simply reinforcing the ego's thought system of opposition.

Why do you need to look at a dinner menu? The Course says you should ask the Holy Spirit what you should do, and that obviously includes what to eat.

Don't tell me you still have insurance policies! Read Lessons 153 and 194 ("In my defenselessness my safety lies."; "I place the future in the Hands of God.").

Don't ask me what I am going to do next week. Read Lesson 135 (which contains the statement: "A healed mind does not plan.").

Why do you lock your car? Read Lesson 181 ("I trust my brothers, who are one with me.").

Etc., etc., etc.!

Throughout all these pronouncements, the student has forgotten, *once again*, that the fourth characteristic of God's teachers—gentleness—means to let go of all harmful thoughts, words, and actions (M-4.IV).

And then there are the attacks masquerading in the form of "whatever we do is all right because we are looking at our egos with Jesus," invoking the opening paragraph of "The 'Dynamics' of the Ego" from Chapter 11 in the text: No one can escape from illusions unless he looks at them..." (T-11.V.1:1). Armed with this weapon, students are able to justify or rationalize all manner of unkind and harmful words and deeds, very similar to the trap couples sometimes fall into, such as: "I am going to be totally honest with you and tell you exactly what I feel." Woe be to the other partner if he or she does not duck in time. Those words should be ample warning that what will follow will be anything *but* honest, let alone loving.

It is clear that to harbor attack thoughts, not to mention act them out in a wish to harm others, must entail the belief—consciously or unconsciously—that the thought system of separation is real. How else could we justify our anger *except* by believing that these objects of our aggression are not only *separate* from us, but also *different*, leading to a mindset that states: "I am right and they are wrong." And so the unkindness that is inevitable by holding on to this perception is also directed at ourselves. As *A Course in Miracles* states:

> You can but hurt yourself. This has been oft repeated, but is difficult to grasp as yet. To minds intent on specialness it is impossible. Yet to those who wish to heal and not attack, it is quite obvious. The purpose of attack is in the mind, and its effects are felt but where it is (T-24.IV.3:1-5).

Or, as we see in two workbook lesson titles:

> I am affected only by my thoughts (W-pII.338).

> I can be hurt by nothing but my thoughts (W-pII.281).

And so the reason we persist in *not* doing the *kind* and *simple* things Jesus asks of us now becomes apparent. To let go of all judgment, belief in differences, and consequently all attack thoughts, means also to let go of the belief in separation. And without that belief in the reality of my *separate* identity from God, and from all other members of the Sonship as well, this ego identity would dissolve. Thus it is "safer" for me to hurt others, because in so doing I am protecting my single, individual self through attack, thereby preserving the ego's thought system of separation and differences from God's living Oneness. As we read in the text:

> If you were one with God and recognized this oneness, you would know His power is yours. But you will not remember this while you believe attack of any kind means anything. It is unjustified in any form, because it has no meaning. The only way it could be justified is if you and your brother were separate from the other, and all were separate from your Creator. For only then would it be possible to attack a part of the creation without the whole, the Son without the Father; and to attack another without yourself, or hurt yourself without the other feeling pain. And this belief you want.... Only the different can attack. So you conclude *because* you can attack, you and your brother must be different (T-22.VI.12:1-6; 13:1-2).

Through such attacks on others, we express our preference to be right rather than happy (T-29.VII.1:9), proving that God is insane for "believing" in perfect oneness, while we are quite sane in our staunchly held position that separation is reality, and being unkind to others is salvation.

We are taught in *A Course in Miracles* that purpose is everything, and that the meaning of anything lies in what it is *for* (T-17.VI.2:2). It is understanding the oft-hidden motivation of self-preservation lying beneath our wish to be unkind that holds the key to Jesus' question as to why we persist in learning not his simple lessons. Stated another way, if "the memory of God comes to the quiet mind" (T-23.I.1:1), then what better way to keep this memory of our oneness in God away from us—thus protecting our separated self—than to keep our minds in a constant state of busyness? Judgment, attack, and idle chatter—the ego's "raucous screams and senseless ravings" (T-21.V.1:6)—are examples of what we have made so natural and turned into a state of perverse comfort for ourselves. Thus our judgmental thoughts and unkind words and actions are indeed quite purposive, serving to keep the peace that forgiveness brings away, the Voice of peace and forgiveness unheard, and forgiveness' ability to lead us back Home rendered forever impotent:

> Gods's peace can never come where anger is, for anger must deny that peace exists. Who sees anger as justified in any way or any circumstance proclaims that peace is meaningless, and

> must believe that it cannot exist. In this condi-
> tion, peace cannot be found.... Returning anger,
> in whatever form, will drop the heavy curtain
> once again, and the belief that peace cannot exist
> will certainly return. War is again accepted as the
> one reality (M-20.3:3-5; 4:2-3).

But one does not need to think of the larger meta-physical consequences, nor even of one's individual salvation, in order to appreciate the *common decency* involved in being kind and helpful to others. To be normal is always a helpful rule of thumb, and a good working definition for "normal" is not going out of one's way to insult, hurt, or in any other way bring harm to one's brethren. It is not necessary that one believe that God did not create the physical universe, for example, to know the importance of treating people with kindness and respect. To be sure, it is not the ultimate healing—which can only occur on the level of the mind—but acting kindly most often reflects the kindness inherent in forgiving oneself, and thus it goes a long way towards leading us to the Home of Kindness itself.

And so, if our goal is truly to awaken from this dream and return Home, then we need to cultivate the very simple practice of remaining vigilant for all our thoughts of hurt and harmfulness, our need to attack and judge. Thus we keep in mind that whenever our peace has left us, and we are tempted to blame others for our disquiet and to exact just punishment for their sin, the ultimate object of our harmfulness is ourselves. And would we truly wish to use another as an instrument whereby *we* deny ourselves entrance into the Kingdom? Especially when the denying agent is *ourself* and *ourself* alone. This is made clear in the following penetrating passage from the text:

> Christ is at God's altar, waiting to welcome His Son. But come wholly without condemnation, for otherwise you will believe that the door is barred and you cannot enter (T-11.IV.6:1-2).

If a person's head were bleeding, for example, and he were told that the pain came from his standing next to a wall and continually banging his head against it, there would be no question—unless the person were severely mentally disturbed—that he would stop. The connection between the *cause*—banging his head against the wall—and the *effect*—the intense pain he was experiencing—would be so clear that he would stop the *cause* instantly so as to remove the *effect.* Jesus makes the same point with us in *A Course in Miracles*—indeed, over and over again. He wants us to understand the direct connection between our unkind thoughts of attack and judgment, and our experienced pain and discomfort. As he says in the text, in the context of choosing to recognize the true cause of the problem of our suffering:

> The choice will not be difficult, because the problem is absurd when clearly seen. No one has difficulty making up his mind to let a simple problem be resolved if it is seen as hurting him, and also very easily removed (T-27.VII.2:5-6).

The problem is that our physical and psychological experience of pain acts as a buffer between the *cause* (in the mind) and *effect* (felt in the body), so that we are not aware of the connection. The true intervening variable—to use the psychological term—between our attack thoughts (the *cause*) and our disquiet (the *effect)* is guilt, and this guilt is almost always unconscious, with but shadowy intimations that from time to time filter through the unconscious barrier into awareness.

It is a fact that guilt is inevitable once we harbor attack thoughts, which the ego always equates with sin. And one of the characteristics of guilt is that it demands punishment. This inner punishment is what ultimately produces our pain and discomfort. But again, since this guilt is out of our awareness, we have no clue as to where our suffering is originating:

> Of one thing you were sure: Of all the many causes you perceived as bringing pain and suffering to you, your guilt was not among them (T-27.VII.7:4).

And without awareness of this connection, there is obviously nothing we can do that would effectively undo the pain and see to it that it never returned. Unnoticed causes, and therefore causes that are not undone, continue to be operative, acting behind the scenes as it were, to ensure that their effects are always there. Thus, all we need do to put an end to our suffering and disquiet is to practice returning to the *cause* of our distress.

> Now you are being shown you *can* escape [from suffering]. All that is needed is you look upon the problem as it is, and not the way that you have set it up (T-27.VII.2:1-2).

And in the context we are discussing here, the cause of our suffering can be identified with our decision to attack others as a means of protecting our unconscious guilt. This withholding of kindness from others, once again, withholds it from ourselves, and thus protects our identity within the dream.

113

Rather than closing the article, as we sometimes do, by citing the Course, perhaps a kind and simple message paraphrased from the master theorist Jiminy Cricket would be in order:

> If you have nothing nice to say, don't say anything at all!

INDEX OF REFERENCES TO *A COURSE IN MIRACLES*

text

text (continued)

workbook for students

manual for teachers

manual for teachers (continued)

clarification of terms

Psychotherapy: Purpose, Process and Practice

The Song of Prayer

The Gifts of God

Foundation for *A Course in Miracles*®

Kenneth Wapnick received his Ph.D. in Clinical Psychology in 1968 from Adelphi University. He was a close friend and associate of Helen Schucman and William Thetford, the two people whose joining together was the immediate stimulus for the scribing of *A Course in Miracles*. Kenneth has been involved with *A Course in Miracles* since 1973, writing, teaching, and integrating its principles with his practice of psychotherapy. He is on the Executive Board of the Foundation for Inner Peace, publishers of *A Course in Miracles*.

In 1983, with his wife Gloria, he began the Foundation for *A Course in Miracles*, and in 1984 this evolved into a Teaching and Healing Center in Crompond, New York, which was quickly outgrown. In 1988 they opened the Academy and Retreat Center in upstate New York. In 1995 they began the Institute for Teaching Inner Peace through *A Course in Miracles*, an educational corporation chartered by the New York State Board of Regents. In 2001 the Foundation moved to Temecula, California. The Foundation publishes a quarterly newsletter, "The Lighthouse," which is available free of charge. The following is Kenneth and Gloria's vision of the Foundation.

In our early years of studying *A Course in Miracles,* as well as teaching and applying its principles in our respective professions of psychotherapy, and teaching and school administration, it seemed evident that this was not the simplest of thought systems to understand. This was so not only in the intellectual grasp of its teachings, but perhaps more importantly in the application of these teachings to our personal lives. Thus, it appeared to us from the beginning that the Course lent itself to teaching, parallel to the ongoing teachings of the Holy Spirit in the daily opportunities within our relationships, which are discussed in the early pages of the manual for teachers.

One day several years ago while Helen Schucman and I (Kenneth) were discussing these ideas, she shared a vision that she had had of a teaching center as a white temple with a gold cross atop it. Although it was clear that this image was symbolic, we understood it to be representative of what the teaching center was to be: a place where the person of Jesus and his message in *A Course in Miracles* would be manifest. We have sometimes seen an image of a lighthouse shining its light into the sea, calling to it those passers-by who sought it. For us, this light is the Course's teaching of forgiveness, which we would hope to share with those who are drawn to the Foundation's form of teaching and its vision of *A Course in Miracles*.

This vision entails the belief that Jesus gave the Course at this particular time in this particular form for several reasons. These include:

1) the necessity of healing the mind of its belief that attack is salvation; this is accomplished through forgiveness, the undoing of our belief in the reality of separation and guilt.

2) emphasizing the importance of Jesus and/or the Holy Spirit as our loving and gentle Teacher, and developing a personal relationship with this Teacher.

3) correcting the errors of Christianity, particularly where it has emphasized suffering, sacrifice, separation, and sacrament as being inherent in God's plan for salvation.

Our thinking has always been inspired by Plato (and his mentor Socrates), both the man and his teachings. Plato's Academy was a place where serious and thoughtful people came to study his philosophy in an atmosphere conducive to their learning, and then returned to their professions to implement what they were taught by the great philosopher. Thus, by integrating abstract philosophical ideals with experience, Plato's school seemed to be the perfect model for the teaching center that we directed for so many years.

We therefore see the Foundation's principal purpose as being to help students of *A Course in Miracles* deepen their understanding of its thought system, conceptually and experientially, so that they may be more effective instruments of Jesus' teaching in their own lives. Since teaching forgiveness without experiencing it is empty, one of the Foundation's specific goals is to help facilitate the process whereby people may be better able to know that their own sins are forgiven and that they are truly loved by God. Thus is the Holy Spirit able to extend His Love through them to others.

Foundation for A Course in Miracles®

Temecula, California

Please see our Web site, www.facim.org, for a complete listing of publications and available translations. You may also write, or call our office for information:

Foundation for *A COURSE IN MIRACLES*®
41397 Buecking Drive
Temecula, CA 92590
(951) 296-6261 • fax (951) 296-5455